YOUNG OFFENDERS AND THE MEDIA

POLICY STUDIES INSTITUTE

The Policy Studies Institute (PSI) is Britain's leading independent research organisation undertaking studies of economic, industrial and social policy, and the workings of political institutions.

PSI is a registered charity, run on a non-profit basis, and is not associated with any political party, pressure group or commercial interest.

PSI attaches great importance to covering a wide range of subject areas with its multi-disciplinary approach. The Institute's 40+ researchers are organised in teams which currently cover the following programmes:

Family Finances – Employment – Information Policy – Social Justice and Social Order – Health Studies and Social Care – Education – Industrial Policy and Futures – Arts and the Cultural Industries – Environment and Quality of Life

This publication arises from the Social Justice programme and is one of over 30 publications made available by the Institute each year.

Information about the work of PSI, and a catalogue of available books can be obtained from:

Marketing Department, PSI 100 Park Village East, London NW1 3SR

YOUNG OFFENDERS AND THE MEDIA
Viewing habits and preferences

Ann Hagell and Tim Newburn

Policy Studies Institute
London

PUBLISHING

The publishing imprint of the independent POLICY STUDIES INSTITUTE 100 Park Village East, London NW1 3SR Telephone: 071-387 2171 Fax: 071-388 0914

ISBN 0 85374 614 1
PSI Research Report 763
A CIP catalogue record of this book is available from the British Library.

1 2 3 4 5 6 7 8 9

PSI publications are available from BEBC Distribution Ltd P O Box 1496, Poole, Dorset, BH12 3YD

Books will normally be despatched within 24 hours. Cheques should be made payable to BEBC Distribution Ltd.

Credit card and telephone/fax orders may be placed on the following freephone numbers:
FREEPHONE: 0800 262260
FREEFAX: 0800 262266

Booktrade representation (UK & Eire): Broadcast Books 24 De Montfort Road, London SW16 1LW Telephone: 081-677 5129

PSI subscriptions are available from PSI's subscription agent Carfax Publishing Company Ltd P O Box 25, Abingdon, Oxford OX14 3UE

Printed and Bound in Great Britain by
Bourne Press Ltd., Bournemouth.

Contents

Lists of Tables and Figures

List of Figures

Acknowledgements

This study was funded jointly by the British Board of Film Classification, the British Broadcasting Corporation, the Broadcasting Standards Council and the Independent Television Commission, and we are grateful to them for their support. Particular thanks go to the following people from those organisations; David Docherty, James Ferman, Margaret Ford, Barrie Gunter, Katherine Lannon, Robin McCron, Andrea Millwood-Hargrave and Guy Phelps.

We are also very grateful to Chris Watkins, Chairman of the National Association for Pastoral Care in Education, for his invaluable help in selecting the sample of schoolchildren and his general support with that element of the research. For reasons of confidentiality, no individual schools can be identified, but we are indebted to all that participated, and we particularly appreciate their co-operation and quick response at a time when many of them were very busy.

Thanks are also due to the police forces and social services departments in the areas that we studied, for their extensive help in gaining access and background information, and to the interviewers (Virginia Bergin, Kevin Dowd, Joe Elliott, Murray Griffin, Ben Hainsworth and Owain Williams) for all their efforts. We also appreciate the support of colleagues in the Social Justice Group at PSI, as well as others at the Institute, who helped in the preparation of this report, particularly Jeremy Eckstein for his advice and Julian McNeelance for administrative assistance.

Finally, thanks must go to all the young people and their families who took part in the research. We are very grateful for their time and interest.

Preface

By James Ferman,
Director, British Board of Film Classification

During the past year, public concern about media violence has surfaced repeatedly in Britain, much of it focused on the possible effects of such violence on the young. The British Board of Film Classification shares that concern, since our policy is based on an awareness that people are, to some extent, what they consume. The possibility that innocence can be corrupted, that human nature can be brutalised by brutal stimuli, is a constant preoccupation of the BBFC.

Board policy on violence has always been clear. We want to protect children from fear, and potential delinquents from anti-social influence. When there appears to be a rise in juvenile crime, we must consider whether screen violence may in some way be linked to it. It would be a failure in responsibility if we did not investigate such links, not just to validate our policy, but to improve it, by helping us to decide just where and how to draw the line.

There have been many attempts to explore the nature of such links, but few have been able to demonstrate a causal relationship. Human nature is far too complex to lend itself to simple explanations. The nature/nurture debate is never-ending, and crucial experiences may have their origin in infancy or adolescence, home or school, family or peer group, or some unique combination of them all. Some of those crucial experiences may have their origin in the thousands of hours of TV or video consumption by the average child, and media regulators must have particular regard to such influences. In the past year, the BBFC has reviewed its policy on violence, as have all those charged with setting standards for British television. And the gathering of evidence is part of that review.

The effects of the mass media can never be looked at in isolation, since we experience them as part of the world we live in, but the untangling of significant influences is a daunting task. And where a child has drifted into a pattern of offending, the nature of those influences may be complex and elusive. When the Board began to look for evidence of the media viewing habits of young offenders, it found that no such study had been done since 1970, long before the advent of video and today's increasingly graphic representations of violence. Cinemas are easy to regulate, since there is a gatekeeper at the box office. But the invention of video and the proliferation of television channels means that most families now have a cinema in their sitting room, and some in their bedrooms as well, with no box office to turn away those under age.

It is tempting to assume that this media-saturated environment must be responsible for changes in behaviour, but there have been worries about juvenile crime at earlier periods in British history when there was no such ready explanation. And despite the pervasive influence of today's media, it is only a small proportion of young people who ever become involved in violent crime. Thus, there must be other factors involved. In the last quarter century, many researchers interested in media effects have begun to approach the problem by looking more closely at the audience - who they are, how they live, what the other influences are on their lives. How do particular individuals use the media, what do they want from it, do they actively seek out certain kinds of excitement or gratification? And how do the other factors in their lives interact with media consumption? This kind of research is essentially descriptive, and it was the starting point we needed if we were ever to relate the consumption of screen violence to the reality of juvenile crime.

In March 1993, the BBFC commissioned the Policy Studies Institute to initiate the first independent research study in more than twenty years into the television and video viewing habits of juvenile offenders. A representative sample was chosen, based on three or more arrests in 1992 of offenders aged between 10 and 17. They were asked to say what they watch, where and how they watch it, and what attracts them to it. We also wanted to know to what extent young people who have been involved in crime actively seek out and enjoy representations of crime or violence.

Since these questions are of vital significance to all the regulatory authorities, the Board was pleased to be joined as co-sponsors of this research by the BBC, the Independent Television Commission, and the Broadcasting Standards Council. The Heads of Research of all these bodies played an active advisory role in designing the study and assessing the findings.

In order to judge the significance of the data about young offenders, it had to be looked at in the context of the rest of their generation. To what extent, for example, are violent films or programmes, or violent video games, actually available to and used by young people in general? Little is known about what secondary school pupils view. For that reason, a parallel survey was undertaken through the National Association for Pastoral Care in Education into the media habits of the teenage population as a whole, so that the viewing patterns of offenders and non-offenders could be compared and contrasted.

The similarities turned out to be more interesting than the differences, particularly given the marked differences in lifestyle. Indeed, finding and interviewing the offenders turned out to be a major problem in itself, and told us a great deal about the family and social backgrounds of those who become involved in juvenile crime. It was the ability of the PSI to investigate the media involvement of each of these juvenile offenders in the context of their specific educational, family and offending histories which makes this research important and, indeed unique.

One point must be clarified. The criminal activities of the offenders which qualified them for inclusion took place in 1992. The interviews took place in the second half of 1993, in some cases more than a year after the commission of the offences, and the interviews were, for the most part, concerned with *current* media habits. Thus, the research could not have been designed to investigate causality. If anything, the data might be seen as investigating the tendency of juveniles already involved in crime - and immersed in chaotic or deprived lifestyles - to seek out certain kinds of entertainment or stimulation. Significant differences might have been anticipated between the viewing habits of offenders and non-offenders commensurate with their markedly different life situations. The extent to which such differences are revealed - or not revealed - makes interesting reading in itself.

This descriptive study is a first step in a long-term commitment to research. The BBFC intends to pursue in some detail any links which may exist between screen violence and real violence. This will involve in-depth interviews of a kind which proved not to be feasible in the present study. It is, in our view, an effort well worth making.

Foreword
By Barrie Gunter
Head of Research, Independent Television Commission

Historically, public anxiety has followed the introduction of any new mass medium of entertainment, particularly when it holds a strong appeal for younger members of the community. Adverse reactions were reported in the nineteenth century when popular romantic and adventure novels first appeared. During the early parts of the twentieth century a similar response was heard following the rapid rise in popularity of motion pictures. In the early 1950s, horror comics were widely criticised and linked to juvenile delinquency. Since then television and lately home video and computer games have been accused of undermining moral values and cultivating a more violent and criminally oriented social climate.

The role played by the mass media in the lives of young people is a recurrent topic of social debate. The audio-visual media (ie, television, video and cinema) especially have been widely criticised for displaying material which is variously judged to be tasteless, psychologically harmful or socially divisive. Sadly, the arguments are not always well-informed. Assumptions about media influences that are founded on flimsy or distorted evidence or misinterpretation of research findings do little to advance the debate in any useful or meaningful sense.

Frequently, statements are made about the role of mass media in shaping public consciousness or conduct which derive from inaccurate or irrelevant research evidence. Failure to consider the significance of the media alongside other social forces and within the familial, educational and cultural contexts which characterise an individual's early upbringing can lead to poorly framed hypotheses and invalid conclusions about the influences of mass media.

It is important to recognise that research into the uses people make of the mass media and how they react to media content comes in different forms. Different research methodologies have varying strengths and weaknesses which need to be taken into account when judging the evidence which derives from them.

One of the key factors in defining the role of media in young people's lives is to establish what use they make of different media. Concerns about levels of delinquency among young people lead to important questions being asked about the causes of this behaviour. The mass media are regularly identified as contributory factors in this context. While ample evidence has been collected over the years about the media habits of children in general, we know much less about the way young offenders use the major mass media.

The study by the Policy Studies Institute which is described in this report has broken new ground by exploring with known young offenders their reported use of different print and audio-visual media. This group has, in turn, been compared with a sample of schoolchildren from the same age group. Although not designed to measure the influences of mass media on young offenders, the study serves to provide preliminary insights into their patterns of media consumption, which represent an important first step in analysing the role played by the media in young offenders' lives.

The results reveal many similarities and some interesting differences between young offenders and schoolchildren in their self-reported media-related behaviours and preferences. The most significant differences reflected important variations in the economic and social circumstances in which each of these groups live. An attempt was also made to flesh out broad descriptive findings about media availability and use with questions about programme and film favourites, and identification with television personalities and movie characters.

As a preliminary exercise this project has been useful insofar as it has provided information about young offenders and their media habits which was lacking before. The research itself reveals nothing abut media influences, but then as a purely descriptive analysis of claimed media-related behaviour it was never designed to do so. No conclusions can or should therefore be derived from it about any role the mass media might play in shaping the personalities or criminal tendencies of young offenders.

Even as a descriptive analysis of media use, its findings should be regarded as indicative rather than as representative. The achieved sample of young offenders fell short of the original target illustrating the difficulties that are to be encountered when attempting to carry out research of this sort with this particular group. This was perhaps one of the most important lessons learned from the exercise.

Looking to the future, there may be some mileage in studying young offenders as a special group in trying to identify whether media content plays an important part in shaping their general character or in triggering specific behaviours. What is likely to be more revealing than self-report evidence of media use, however, would be an analysis of any idiosyncratic modes of responding to media content. A more clinical style of interview might be recommended in which the confidence and relaxed attention of interviewees is more effectively established. As well as examining the use young offenders make of mass media, we need to know more about how they react to different kinds of media content.

Chapter 1 **Introduction**

Background

For as long as television has existed, there have been those who question the content and quality of the visual images that can be broadcast into the homes of the general public. Indeed, in the 1960s, a pressure group (originally called the 'Clean-up TV Campaign', and later the National Viewers' and Listeners' Association) was formed, one of whose central aims was to campaign for greater control over what its members perceived to be the excessive - and increasing - amount of violence and sex being broadcast.

The development of video technology, and its rapid spread in the early 1980s, increased the options open to the viewer, and gave rise to concern that the system used to restrict access to cinema films could be easily bypassed by unscrupulous video merchants. There emerged what might reasonably be termed a 'moral panic' in 1983 about the prevalence of so-called 'video nasties', and the ease with which young children could get hold of such material[1]. Such concern led to the passing of the Video Recordings Act 1984 - a Private Member's Bill sponsored by Graham Bright MP[2]. Under the Act, the Home Secretary can designate any person as the authority responsible for the classification of video films. In practice, this has been the British Board of Film Classification (BBFC).

Despite the introduction and implementation of new procedures for the control of such material, worries about the content of cinema films, video films and television programmes have recently surfaced once again. The Parliamentary Office of Science and Technology recently summarised the concerns surrounding the ever-developing viewing technology:

"Technology has transformed home entertainment via video recorders, satellite and cable TV, while special effects technology allows murders etc. to be shown in `realistic' detail in settings from science fiction through `teenage terror' movies to thrillers or `action' dramas. On the news, portable cameras and satellite links bring the graphic detail of distant events straight into the home. Technology has also changed viewing habits. Films are now viewed more via videos and TV than in the cinema, while home computers and video games can create an additional route for violent material".[3]

Most recently, the issue has been linked to current concerns about juvenile offenders. Actors have joined the debate; Sir Anthony Hopkins, the star of one of the films that caused much recent disquiet (*The Silence of the Lambs*), has suggested that he is perturbed by the possible effect of such films. Such a position is far from novel, however. Concerns about the likely impact of specific films litter British film history[4], with Stanley Kubrick's withdrawal of his film A *Clockwork Orange* remaining perhaps the most notorious of all.

Despite the limited scope of this descriptive project, a study investigating the offending behaviour and viewing habits of children will inevitably be linked to the vast research literature on the role of media consumption in antisocial behaviour[5]. However, despite the large number of research studies addressing the general issue, the lack of consensus arising from previous work over the links between violence on the screen and aggressive behaviour in viewers has resulted in discussions concerning young offenders and their media use being frequently conducted at the level of assertion and assumption.

Particularly with reference to young offenders, there is a lack of basic descriptive information about what these teenagers choose to watch, how much they watch, to what extent *violent* films are actually viewed by such young people, and whether they actively seek out, watch and enjoy representations of criminal activities. Centrally for the purposes of this report, it is important to consider whether their viewing habits are significantly different from non-offenders of the same age. By addressing these descriptive aims, this project can only contribute to the discussion about links between offending and viewing in two specific ways. In the first instance, it has been suggested that heavy (or heavier than average) viewing of television (and thus, television violence) is associated with offending. It is hypothesised, for example, by those who make this suggestion, that one link may be through some form of desensitisation. The more violence viewed, the more "dulled" responses to violence might become, allowing increased tolerance of violence by the viewer. Others have suggested that imitation or disinhibition form the link. While this research project cannot test such theories, it is able to examine whether those with unusually high rates of recorded offending are prone to watch a greater amount of violent television than those without equivalent levels of offending.

Second, although the research literature has largely confined itself to the question of a relationship between television violence and teenage aggression, there has been an assumption in the mass media that television programming and Hollywood studio output are somehow responsible for what are held to be higher rates of juvenile offending. The difficulty with this argument is that the majority of juvenile offending is not violent. Murder by young children or teenagers is extremely rare, a fact that contributes to the massive press coverage when it does occur. Very little, if anything, is known about the possibility that there might be a link between general juvenile offending and media viewing habits.

The small research study described in this report provides some background information in relation to these questions. It focuses on a group of juvenile offenders, explores aspects of their television and video viewing habits, and compares them to those of a sample of schoolchildren. It should be emphasized at this point that this is a limited piece of work, and that consideration of possible links between viewing habits and criminal behaviour is not within its scope. If this research were to uncover any association between offending and viewing preferences, it would still not be possible to draw conclusions concerning <u>causality</u> from the data collected as part of this study. Such a question has to remain the province of further, much more ambitious research. This report is simply intended to provide background information on which to base a more balanced discussion of the viewing of crime and violence by young offenders.

Research Aims

The study draws on interviews with 78 juvenile offenders aged between 12 and 18, and a questionnaire survey of a representative sample of 538 schoolchildren from a similar age range. With reference to television, cinema, video viewing, and use of computer games, the study attempted to address the following questions:-

(1) Are there differences in the viewing habits of young offenders when compared to their peers? Are they watching more or less than other teenagers? Do they watch television and view films at different times of the day to other teenagers?

(2) Are there any differences in the viewing preferences of young offenders, compared with children of the same age? Do they choose to watch different television programmes or films from schoolchildren in general? Do young offenders prefer to watch more violent films than their peers, and to what extent do children in general watch violent films? Do different types of offence patterns relate to different viewing preferences?

(3) What is the familial and social context of offenders' lives? How do television and film viewing fit into these lives?

(4) Given the rising media concern with what some suggest to be the potentially addictive nature of video games, and their violent content, is there any variation between the offenders and other teenagers in the preference for, or playing of, particular video games?

Notes
1. For a longer discussion see, for example, Barker, M. (1984) (Ed) *The Video Nasties: Freedom and Censorship in the Media* London: Pluto Press.

2. The background to this and other similar concerns are covered in greater detail in Newburn, T. (1991) *Permission and Regulation: Law and Morals in Post-war Britain*. London: Routledge.

3. Parliamentary Office of Science and Technology (1993) *The Psychologist*, August 1993, p353-356.

4. See *inter alia*, Phelps, G. (1975) *Film Censorship* London: Gollancz; Trevelyan, J. (1973) *What the Censor Saw*, London: Michael Joseph; Wistrich, E. (1978) *I Don't Mind the Sex, It's the Violence* London: Marion Boyars.

5. See, for example, reviews such as Cumberbatch, G. and Howitt, D. *A Measure of Uncertainty: The Effects of the Mass Media*, London: John Libbey and Co Ltd, and Wartella, E. (1994, in press) 'Media and the problem behaviours of adolescents' in Rutter, M. and Smith, D.J. (Eds) *Psychosocial Disorders of Youth: A Study of Cross-National Trends and their Causes*, London: Wiley.

Chapter 2 Study description and sample characteristics

Overall Design

This study focused on comparisons between two groups; a group of juvenile offenders and a representative sample of schoolchildren. Both groups were asked the same questions about their viewing habits and preferences. With the offenders, these questions took the form of an interview conducted in the young person's home or wherever they were living. The schoolchildren completed a confidential questionnaire containing the same questions, administered in their classrooms by their teachers.

Sample Selection

Young Offenders

A large minority of children will get into trouble with the police at some point in their lives and this will usually be in the middle of their teens; the peak age for participation in offending for boys, for example, is 15 years-old[1]. Indeed, it is well established that approximately a third of adult males will have been convicted of at least one offence by their thirties[2], and most of these convictions will have been as a result of offences committed whilst they were juveniles[3]. However, the majority of these young people will only be involved in minor criminal activities and then probably only for a short period of time. As the central purpose of this study was to compare offenders with schoolchildren, it was felt to be important that the major focus be on the more severe or more frequent end of juvenile offending. Consequently, the selection of cases for interview concentrated on juveniles who had been charged or cautioned by the police a minimum of three times within one calendar year. The juvenile offenders were selected from two geographical areas - a Midlands county and two London boroughs.

These areas were chosen for practical rather than theoretical reasons; they were accessible for research personnel, information on official offending was centrally recorded, and the two areas combined covered a spread of rural and city populations. In these areas, a total of 531 juveniles (between 10 and 17 years old in 1992) were identified who, according to their police records, had been arrested three times or more in 1992.

From this sample, over two hundred were selected for interview. The child's and parents' addresses were drawn from official files. The majority of sample members were still under eighteen years of age at the start of the interviewing period in the middle of 1993, and consequently, permission had to be sought before contacting the children. Once this had been given, the young person was approached and asked if they would be willing to take part. A proportion of the young people (approximately 17 per cent) were in some form of custody or in children's home, in which case permission was also sought from the Director or Governor of the institution or home.

Although the interview itself was well received by those who took part, a substantial proportion of the original sample proved to be extremely difficult to locate, or to interview once located. This was, however, not surprising given the nature of the sample as a whole, who were prone to frequent changes of address and, in some cases, were actively seeking to avoid being contacted by 'official' agencies, either because of the offending behaviour of family members or because of debts. Difficulties were encountered in finding the family in the first place; in gaining the co-operation of the family once traced; in finding the child after gaining parental permission (on many occasions, parents did not know where the child was living, or when he or she would be home), and in getting the child to be present at a particular time.

Table 2.1 summarises the numbers of young people included in the sample. Full interviews were conducted with 75 of these offenders. In addition, three further offenders were interviewed at one children's home during a research visit to see another child. These additional children were also frequent offenders. Thus, interview data were available on 78 offenders. Officially recorded police information was available on 71 of those, and partial information on the remaining seven. Of these 78 frequent offenders, nine were girls and 69 were boys. They were aged between 12 and 18 at the time of interview, with an average age of just over 15 and a half years.

Table 2.1: Number of young offenders and comparison schoolchildren included in the study

	Boys		Girls		Total
Group	n	%	n	%	n
Young Offenders	69	(88.5)	9	(11.5)	78
Comparison Schoolchildren	476	(88.5)	62	(11.5)	538

Schoolchildren

In order to draw any conclusions about the viewing habits of these young offenders, it was essential that they were compared to the viewing habits of an ordinary cross-section of teenagers. In order to achieve this, PSI liaised with the National Association for Pastoral Care in Education (NAPCE). Several thousand secondary schools are members of NAPCE, and its membership covers the whole range of types of secondary education available in England. From NAPCE's lists, 92 schools were selected for approach, chosen randomly from the full list of members. Each of these schools received a letter from PSI and a covering letter from NAPCE, requesting their co-operation in the research. They were asked to administer questionnaires to up to approximately 50 schoolchildren from a specified year group. The teachers were instructed not to select special classes, but to choose a representative group. The schoolchildren did not have to put their names on the questionnaires, so neither the teachers nor the research team knew the identity of respondents. Instructions on administering the questionnaire were included, as well as a short questionnaire directed at the teacher, containing questions about the type of school, number of children, and age ranges covered. This was included as an additional check that the replying schools were reasonably representative of the original list. However, apart from this basic information, confidentiality was assured and schools were not asked to identify themselves or the children in their replies. It was hoped that this would reassure the children and the schools that they would not be personally singled out for attention.

Of the 92 schools approached, 60 returned questionnaires, (a response rate of 65 per cent) many more than had been originally anticipated. This is a very high response rate for a postal survey that did not include any telephone contact with the respondents or any follow-up letters, and we are reasonably confident that the schools that replied were representative of the 92 approached. However, as the schools were approached at the end of the summer term, it was inevitable that the children still attending school at that time were the younger children and, in addition, schools did not comply in every case with our requests for the questionnaire to be given to specific age groups. In such cases, the tendency was for the questionnaire to be administered in classes at the lower end of the age range. Nevertheless, approximately 1000 children (out of over 2500 who replied) fell within the age range of the offenders. Half of these were girls, whereas the ratio within the offenders was 1:8 girls to boys. Therefore, a random sample of the schoolgirl respondents was taken, in order that the sex ratio within the schools sample was equal to that within the offender sample. This resulted in a sample of 538 schoolchildren, consisting of 476 boys and 62 girls. Although the age range of both samples was the same, the mean age of the schoolchildren was just over 14 and a half, making them approximately one year younger on average than the sample of offenders. Thus, the offenders and the schoolchildren were approximately matched for age, and for sex ratios within the two groups. However, no matching was possible on any other variables including, for example, socio-economic status or ethnicity. In the case of socio-economic status, matching would be very difficult in practice, as offenders will tend to come from backgrounds with lower than average family income. In the case of ethnicity, the offender sample was drawn largely from an area with very low overall numbers of people from ethnic minorities, and the sample was, consequently, mostly white. The ethnicity of the schoolchildren is unknown.

Sample Representativeness

A variety of efforts were made to ensure the representativeness of the schoolchildren. The range of schools covered within NAPCE, the randomness of the sample of schools from this range, and the high response rate from the schools contacted, all go some way to confirming the representativeness of this sample of 538 schoolchildren. Given that the questionnaire was administered in schools towards the end of the summer term, in most cases after exams were over, the schoolchildren were most likely to be those who were regular attenders and, thus, most unlike the 'regular offenders' with whom they were compared. Thus, were it the case that young offenders' viewing habits were significantly different from those of young people in general, it is likely that they would have been revealed by the comparisons made in this study. In fact, the chances of finding differences between the schoolchildren and the offenders were likely to be enhanced as we could not control for variables such as socio-economic status.

Despite the low response rates, the 78 young offenders represent an unusual and extreme sample. As far as we are aware, no other studies of viewing habits have addressed their questions to a group of this size, comprising the most frequent offenders in the areas from which they were selected. The difficulties experienced in contacting these offenders reflect the unusualness and value of the sample. The only comparable exercises conducted by others in the field have been informal conversations or qualitative studies with much smaller groups of offenders. Nonetheless, drawing firm conclusions from a sample size of 78 should be resisted, and these data must be regarded as exploratory and illustrative due to the relatively few offenders seen. However, as a sample of very frequent offenders, this group offer a rare and unique opportunity to investigate viewing habits.

Given the low response rate of the offenders, however, it is worth considering how representative these 78 juvenile offenders were of the larger group of all 531 juveniles arrested three times or more in their areas. Checks on offending rates, arrest rates, sex ratios, ethnicity (the vast majority of offenders were white) and age suggested that the interviewed offenders did not differ significantly from the larger group of all frequent offenders in any important respect[4]. We are confident therefore that both the sample of schoolchildren and the sample of offenders were reasonably representative of the two very different populations from which they were drawn.

The Schools Questionnaire

The schools questionnaire was a short self-completion booklet, designed to be completed without any additional instructions from teachers. A copy is included in Appendix 1. The cover notes stressed confidentiality and as no space was provided for respondents to write their names, they were discouraged from identifying themselves. It was introduced as a "Leisure Activities Survey", the purpose of which was to look at what programmes and films young people are watching on video and television, and at the cinema. It was suggested that a large number of schools were taking part, but there was no mention of offenders. The majority of questions required a tick in a box as the reply; for the open-ended questions respondents had to write names of people, titles of films, or reasons for choices. It was important that it would not present any reading challenge to the full age range of respondents and so was designed to be as simple as possible. Questions covered reading habits (comics, magazines and newspapers), general access to television and other media, television preferences and viewing habits, cinema and video film preferences and viewing habits, and use of computer games. It took approximately twenty minutes to complete.

The Young Offenders Interview

The interviews with the young offenders were set up and conducted by a total of six interviewers, and the first author. Five were young men, and all were experienced interviewers. After several background questions concerning living circumstances, the interviewers followed the largely structured interview schedule, which included a small proportion of open-ended questions, and took approximately 15 minutes to complete. A full copy is included in Appendix 2. Questions paralleled those in the schools questionnaire, and the order was identical to the ordering of questions in the schools questionnaire.

In both cases, with the group of schoolchildren and with the group of offenders, it was the case that data collection relied exclusively on the childrens' own reports of their viewing habits and preferences. There were no measures of actual viewing behaviour available. The responses to the questions were therefore open to the biases always present in self- report data.

Background information on the young offenders sample

Average numbers of arrests and offences

Full official information on all arrests and offending during 1992 was available on 71 (91 per cent) of the 78 offenders included in the study. For the remaining seven, partial background information was collected. These remaining seven interviewees were not particularly different from those on whom full data were available, and their partial information confirmed that they were also frequent offenders.

The 71 offenders for whom full data were available had been arrested, on average, between four and five times in 1992, approximately six months to a year before interviewing took place (Table 2.2). The highest number of arrests in 1992 for any one individual was 18. These were all arrests that subsequently resulted in further police action; many respondents may also have been arrested but subsequently not processed by the police, so these figures are likely to be an understatement of total arrests for these offenders in 1992. The majority of them were still offending at the time of the interview and a proportion were seen in custody, as mentioned above. Many had begun offending before 1992. By their own accounts, half of the respondents reported that they had first been arrested at or before the age of 12. Since their average age at interview was 15 and a half, many had accumulated long police records during their teenage years, of which the data for 1992 reflect only a part.

According to police files, these 71 offenders accounted for over 750 offences between them in 1992. These offences included all that were known to have been committed by these offenders which ended in conviction or caution, as well as offences alleged (by the police) to have been committed by them, which were subsequently discontinued or dismissed by the police, the Crown Prosecution Service or the courts. They also included offences for which the juvenile admitted guilt, but which were 'taken into consideration' by a court when sentencing, rather than being prosecuted separately. Table 2.2 summarises the numbers of arrests and offences per offender. On average, each offender had seven known or alleged offences in 1992, and an average of 3.5 offences each that had been 'taken into consideration' by a court, together giving an average 10.8 offences per offender.

Table 2.2: Average numbers of arrests and offences per offender in 1992

	Average number per offender
Arrests in 1992	4.5
Total known or alleged offences in 1992	10.8

Figure 2.1 portrays the actual number of offences attributed to each offender, showing that the range of offences in this group ranged between one and less than 70. The upper categories on the figure are collapsed for ease of presentation. The maximum number of known and alleged offences committed by any one offender in 1992 was 63. The sole offender with only one offence

was arrested three times, but his police file only recorded this one incident. This may have reflected a time-lag in the details of his offences reaching his police file.

Figure 2.1: Number of offences per offender

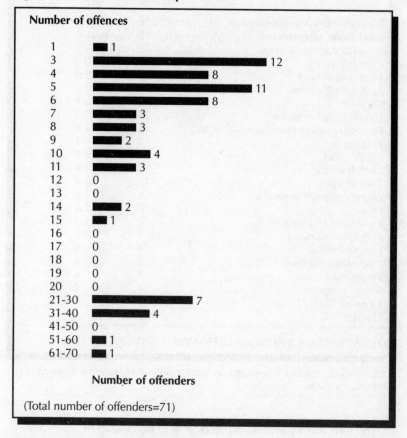

Number of offences

Number of offences	Number of offenders
1	1
3	12
4	8
5	11
6	8
7	3
8	3
9	2
10	4
11	3
12	0
13	0
14	2
15	1
16	0
17	0
18	0
19	0
20	0
21-30	7
31-40	4
41-50	0
51-60	1
61-70	1

Number of offenders

(Total number of offenders=71)

Types of offences committed

Most juvenile offending tends to involve high proportions of theft, non- residential burglary and car crime. The young offenders included in this study committed a wide range of offences, but their offences were broadly representative of juvenile crime as a whole. Table 2.3 presents an overall summary of all the known and alleged offences that they committed between them in 1992, categorised by type. This table excludes offences 'taken into consideration', as it was frequently difficult to classify them by type.

Table 2.3: Numbers of different types of offences committed by sample members in 1992

Offence types	Numbers committed in 1992	Per cent
Burglary-other & unspecified	76	15.2
Road Traffic offences	55	11.0
Criminal damage & arson	52	10.4
Theft from shop	50	10.0
Theft unspecified	45	9.0
Actual bodily harm	39	7.8
Car theft	32	6.4
Handling stolen goods	27	5.4
Procedural offences (breach of bail,etc)	23	4.6
Robbery	22	4.4
Public order	14	2.8
Theft from car	14	2.8
Theft of cycle	12	2.4
Going equipped to steal	8	1.6
Other	7	1.4
Possession of a weapon	7	1.4
Burglary-residential	6	1.2
Drugs offences	4	.8
Aggravated car theft	2	.4
Prostitution	2	.4
Sexual offences	2	.4
Grievous bodily harm	1	.2
Unclassified	1	.2
TOTAL KNOWN & ALLEGED OFFENCES*	501	(100.0%)

* Excluding offences 'taken into consideration', where offence types were not always given.

The four most common offences within this group of 71 frequent offenders (with full police information) were non-residential burglary (15.2 per cent), road traffic offences (such as driving without a licence, without tax, without due care and attention, etc, 11 per cent), criminal damage (10.4 per cent), and theft from shops (10 per cent).

Most of the offenders had committed a variety of different offences, and there was little evidence of any tendency to specialise in one particular area of crime. For this reason, the offenders will generally be treated as a whole group, and subdivisions will not be made on the basis of offence type. A further reason for not dividing the group was that these figures only represent data from one year of these young peoples' offending careers, and it is possible that those who were not convicted of certain offences one year, had been in the previous or subsequent years. In addition, there is, inevitably, a wide division between officially recorded juvenile offending and self-reported juvenile offending[5], and the fact that a young person is not actually convicted of a certain crime does not imply that he or she has not committed it. However, there is one exception to this rule regarding sub-dividing the group; in a later chapter (Chapter 4) the group will be divided into two for the purposes of one set of analyses of viewing preferences, based on whether or not they were convicted of any violent offences.

The importance of this discussion of offence numbers and type is that it serves to illustrate the fact that this was a fairly extreme group of juvenile offenders. They had all been arrested several times during the course of one year and had or were alleged to have committed a large number of offences during that period. They had had substantial involvement with the criminal justice system, and could quite justifiably be described as representing the heavy end of juvenile offending. However, the table demonstrates the lack of very serious violent crime among frequent offenders, as there are no cases of murder, manslaughter or rape in the sample.

Notes

1. Tarling, R. (1993) *Measuring Offending* London: HMSO.

2. Home Office Statistical Department (1985), *Criminal Careers of those born in 1953, 1958, 1963*. Statistical Bulletin 7/85 London: Home Office Statistical Department.

3. Farrington, D.P (1986) 'Age and Crime'. In Tonry, M. and Morris, N. (Eds) *Crime and Justice* Vol 7, Chicago: University of Chicago Press.

4. However, interviewing had been targeted at the most frequent offenders in the group. Although those interviewed were representative of the whole group, there were some differences between those chosen for

interviewing and subsequently seen, and those chosen but who could not subsequently be interviewed for one reason or another. It was slightly more difficult to interview the most frequent offenders.

5. See Hagell, A. and Newburn, T. (1994) *Persistent Young Offenders*, London: PSI, for a further discussion of the difference between self- reported and officially recorded juvenile offending.

Chapter 3   Written and visual media use

To what extent do young offenders and comparison schoolchildren like and use different types of media? Do they prefer different programmes, do they see different films, do they vary in their attachment to computer games? This chapter will present basic descriptive information on the written and visual media use of the two groups.

Comics, Magazines and Newspapers

Looking first at reading habits, the most striking difference between the samples lay not in *what* they read, but in the proportions that said that they read a comic or magazine regularly. Reading did not appear to be a popular activity among the sample of offenders, of whom 64 per cent said that they did not read a magazine or a comic *regularly*. Among the schoolchildren, only eight per cent said that they did not read any comic or magazine regularly. Viewed in the light of the well established overlap between juvenile offending, behaviour problems and reading difficulties[1], it was perhaps not surprising that such a high proportion of the offenders were not reading regularly. By their own admission in answer to background questions, a quarter of these offenders had reading problems and approximately one in eight had had remedial help at school.

If they were reading comics and magazines, the most popular titles that were read regularly by the male offenders were sports magazines (*Football Monthly, Match, Shoot etc*) followed closely by traditional comics such as the *Beano, Dandy* and so forth - comics not generally associated with children of this age. Music magazines were more common among the female offenders as were titles aimed at the women's market such as *Just Seventeen* and *Marie Claire*. A small minority

of the male offenders (5 of the 69) said that they read more adult oriented titles such as *Viz, Zit* and *Acne* on a regular basis. Among the schoolchildren, the boys' most popular titles were those connected with computers and sport, whilst the girls again reported reading magazines specifically aimed at young women (particularly *Just Seventeen,* and *Mizz*) and music magazines such as *Smash Hits.* Nearly 11 per cent of the schoolboys claimed to read *Viz* or similar magazines regularly. More importantly perhaps, the titles that have in the past been the subject of public concern such as *Gun Mart, Guns and Weapons, Combat and Survival,* and soft porn magazines such as *Penthouse, Men Only* and *Fiesta* were mentioned on occasion by a very small number of schoolboys but not mentioned at all by the offenders.

As far as newspapers were concerned, the tendency was again for the offenders to report that they were reading less than the schoolchildren. Although similar proportions of schoolchildren and offenders said that they read a newspaper 'every day', a third of the offenders said they 'hardly ever' or 'never' read a newspaper compared to only one tenth of the schoolchildren (see Table 3.1).

Table 3.1: Frequency of Newspaper Reading

	Schoolchildren %	Offenders %
Every day	46	44
More than once a week	23	1
Once a week	16	8
Less than once a week	5	13
Hardly ever/never	10	34

The range of newspapers read was predictably wide, though only a small proportion of the schoolchildren claimed to read a broadsheet newspaper often, and none of the young offenders did so (see Figure 3.1). One third of the schoolchildren said that they read their local newspaper most frequently, and over half mentioned one of the national tabloids. Three-quarters of the offenders said that they read one of the tabloids most frequently, a third mentioning *The Sun*.

Figure 3.1: Choice of newspaper

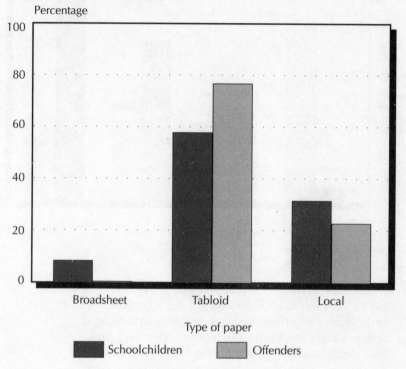

Percentage

Type of paper

■ Schoolchildren   ▢ Offenders

Access to Television

The children in the study were asked a series of questions about the equipment to which they had access. In terms of the reported number of televisions in the household there was a dramatic difference between the schoolchildren and the young offenders. For example, only three per cent of the schoolchildren said that there was only one television in their household compared to over a third of offenders. Reinforcing this disparity, almost one half of the schoolchildren said that there were more than three televisions in their household, compared to 16 per cent of the offenders (see Figure 3.2).

Figure 3.2: Televisions in the household

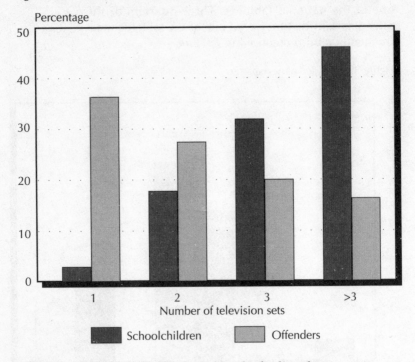

This general trend was reinforced by the finding that over three-quarters (78 per cent) of the schoolchildren in the study had a television in their bedroom compared with just under half of the offenders (49 per cent). Thus, the offenders, although comparing favourably with the 13-14 year- olds in Gunter et al's (1991) study of children's views of television, of whom 48 per cent claimed to have a television in their bedroom[2], are disadvantaged when compared to the children in this study. Either the schoolchildren in this study were relatively privileged, or things have changed since Gunter et al's 1991 survey, and children now have more access than three years ago. The differences were less marked for other forms of equipment (radios, video cassette recorders, and compact disc player or stereo equipment) where coverage in the general population is anyway very high. In all cases a higher proportion of the schoolchildren than the offenders reported having such equipment in their household, though the differences were not especially large (see Table 3.2).

Table 3.2: Equipment in the household

Type of Equipment	Schoolchildren %	Offenders %
Video Cassette Recorder[3]	94	82
Radio	98	85
Compact Disc, other stereo equip.	97	89

The same pattern applied to access to non-terrestrial broadcasting channels. The schoolchildren had higher rates of access although the differences were consistent but not huge (see Figure 3.3).

Figure 3.3: Access to satellite TV channels in the household

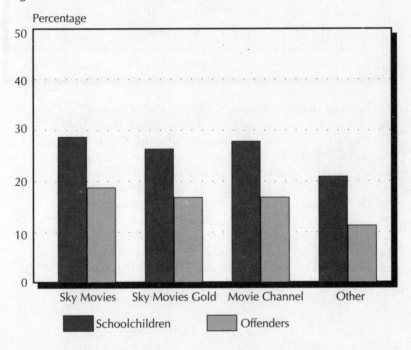

It should be noted that of those 17 per cent of offenders who were seen in custody or Local Authority care, all had access to television and films, but this was necessarily limited, depending on their placement.

Frequency and Amount of Television Viewed

Offenders and schoolchildren were asked to estimate how many hours of television they watched on (a) an average weekday, (b) an average Saturday and (c) an average Sunday. Table 3.3 summarises their responses.

Table 3.3: Amount of television viewed on average days

	Average weekday viewing		Average Saturday viewing		Average Sunday viewing	
	School children	Offenders	School children	Offenders	School children	Offenders
None	1.5%	2.7%	5.4%	10.7%	10.4%	17.3%
< 4 hours	51.0%	49.0%	33.5%	41.3%	48.5%	33.3%
4-6 hours	39.5%	25.3%	47.1%	33.3%	35.0%	25.3%
>6 hours	8.0%	22.7%	14.0%	14.7%	8.9%	24.0%

The results to questions such as these, asking viewers to estimate the amount of television watched, should be treated with a certain amount of caution. It is notoriously difficult to assess hours of television viewing accurately in retrospect and, in addition, respondents were not asked to distinguish between viewing of terrestrial broadcasts and viewing of cable and satellite programmes. It is also probable that respondents will have been confused sometimes about the distinction between programmes watched on television and pre-recorded films viewed on television. It is likely that their estimates will be over-inclusive, covering several different types of output viewed on the television screen.

A slightly larger proportion of offenders than schoolchildren reported either that they watched no television or that they watched a great deal of television. Thus, twice as many offenders reported that they watched no television on Saturdays compared with the schoolchildren, while over twice as many offenders reported watching more than six hours on weekdays compared with the schoolchildren. Similarly, more offenders than schoolchildren reported that they saw no television on Sundays, yet nearly three times as many offenders as schoolchildren reported that they watched television for more than six hours on Sundays.

This complicated pattern of results, and the reservations expressed concerning the small number of children in the offending group, makes it difficult to draw firm conclusions about differences in the viewing habits of the samples. In addition, in making comparisons of this type, it is important to point out the differences in lifestyles of the two groups. By definition, all of the children in the comparison group were attending school, whereas only one third of the offenders were still in full-time education at the time of interview, and of those offenders not at school, many were unemployed. Thus, many of the offenders had no day-time commitments at all, and so therefore had fewer constraints on when they could watch television. In support of this, an overall comparison of the number of time periods during the week and weekend when television was viewed suggested that the offenders were watching television on a slightly greater number of separate time periods than the schoolchildren. This might be a better estimate than asking for approximations of number of hours viewed. To assess the number of time periods during which television was viewed, an average day was divided into five periods. Respondents estimated how many periods they had watched television on average weekdays, Saturdays and Sundays. The offenders reported that they watched during an average of 15 (out of the 35 possible) time periods during the week, while the schoolchildren reported watching during 13 time periods. Given the difficulty of assessing how much television has been viewed, and the differences in lifestyles, these differences are unlikely to be of great importance. However, one striking difference emerged when an analysis of late night television viewing was conducted. The proportions of schoolchildren and offenders viewing television during the 9pm-11pm and the 11pm-6.30am time periods were compared. The results are presented in Table 3.4, which demonstrates that there were no differences in the proportions of each group viewing directly after the 9pm watershed, but the offenders were more likely to be viewing during the very late hours of the evening, and the early hours of the morning.

Table 3.4: Late night television viewing

Late night television viewing			
	Weekdays	Saturdays	Sundays
9pm-11pm	%	%	%
Schoolchildren	59	65	53
Offenders	62	46	54
11pm-6.30am			
Schoolchildren	7	27	10
Offenders	51	43	42

To conclude, these offenders were not viewing substantially more television whichever viewing assessment is used, but there was some evidence that they were viewing television at different times than the schoolchildren. The following section examines whether the offenders tend to watch different types of programmes.

Preferences for Particular Television Programmes

The two samples were asked to name their five favourite television programmes. Among the male offenders a significant minority (16 per cent) said that they did not have a favourite programme. Among the group that did feel able to answer this question by far the most popular programmes were soap operas (see Table 3.5). There were four in particular that were nominated by between 35 per cent and 46 per cent of the male offenders - *The Bill* (46 per cent), *Eastenders* (41 per cent), *Neighbours* (41 per cent) and *Home and Away* (35 per cent). *Prisoner Cell*

Block H was the fifth most popular. The majority of the rest of the programmes mentioned were sports programmes (*Match of the Day, Sportsnight*), Sitcoms (*Birds of a Feather, The Cosby Show*) and comedy shows (*Blackadder, Cheers, Bottom*). A similar pattern emerged among the young female offenders, who frequently selected *Home and Away, Eastenders* and *Neighbours* as their favourite programmes.

Table 3.5: Favourite Television Programmes (top five)

	Offenders		School children	
	Boys	Girls	Boys	Girls
1	The Bill	Home & Away	Home & Away	Home & Away
3	Neighbours	Neighbours	The Bill	Eastenders
4	Home & Away	-[4]	Quantum Leap	Brookside
5	Prisoner Cell Block H	-	Eastenders	Roseanne

Among the schoolchildren, soap operas were also by far the most popular programmes. Over a half (56 per cent) of the schoolgirls listed *Home and Away* as one of their favourite programmes, as did over one third (34 per cent) of the schoolboys. *Neighbours* was the second most popular programme, nominated by 55 per cent of the girls and 26 per cent of the boys, followed by *Eastenders* for the girls (35 per cent) and *The Bill* for the boys (22 per cent). In short, Table 3.6 suggests that, although the choices made by the offenders were not identical to those being made by the comparison group of schoolchildren, they were broadly similar.

Nevertheless, in spite of the fact that the naming of favourite programmes did not differ greatly between the two groups, it is the case that the proportions naming one programme rather than another varied. Thus, for example, approaching twice as many male offenders as male schoolchildren named *Neighbours* (41 per cent against 26 per cent of the boys in the two samples).

Similarly, not only did the offending boys rank *The Bill* at the top of their list, but a higher proportion of them (46 per cent) selected it amongst their favourites compared with the schoolboys (22 per cent). However, given the small sample size of the offenders, it is probably more circumspect to err on the side of caution and concentrate on rankings and stated preferences rather than on precise proportions.

Soap operas were, then, dominant among the choices made by both the schoolchildren and the offenders. Not only did the genre dominate but, by and large, it was the same titles that were chosen by each of the groups. Much of the literature on soap operas has been concerned with the extent to which such programmes offer opportunities for escape or, alternatively, for identification with the characters or the story-line. As will be suggested below, relatively few of the offenders - boys or girls - seemed to identify with people appearing on television generally, and they did so even less frequently with characters in their favourite soaps. They did, however, suggest that certain of the programmes contained a degree of realism that made them attractive. This was especially the case amongst the male offenders whose favourite programme was *The Bill*. What was common in the reasons given for many of the offenders' choices of favourite programmes, including *The Bill*, was 'action':

> "Because they chase cars" (*The Bill*)
> "Fires and action" (*London's Burning*)
> "All the things that happen in it - violence, killing, punching, all sorts" (*Prisoner Cell Block H*)

The finding that it was *The Bill* that was the runaway favourite among the offenders may have reflected the particular programme's ability to connect with experiences that were meaningful within the context of their lives in general. There is no shortage of broadcast drama in which the police play a central part, yet it was those programmes which were perceived by the offenders to come closest to what they experienced as 'reality' that were most popular. Thus, programmes like *Crimewatch UK* attracted quite a lot of interest among the offenders, whereas American police-based dramas did not. The offenders were careful to distinguish between those soap operas that they felt were 'believable' and others whose realism they felt was doubtful. Perhaps the major attraction of *The Bill*, for example, was for many of the offenders the extent to which it reflected things they recognised, they understood, or things that they thought might be helpful to them:

> "*The Bill* - I like watching the police to see if it's real"
> "It's the closest to life you'll get" (*The Bill*)
> "*The Bill* is real, but the rest is just enjoyable"
> "Because of the police...to work out what not to do - so that I don't get caught." (*The Bill*)

With the exception of *Eastenders* the rest of the popular soaps - *Home and Away* and *Neighbours* in particular - were more a source of escapism, and were especially attractive because of their continuing storyline:

> "I like the stories. It's a series - I like following what happens to people" (*Neighbours*)
> "It's a laugh - so fake (*Prisoner Cell Block H*). *Neighbours* is fake, but the story is exciting. *Home and Away* is the same"
> "Habit. I watched them from the beginning so I watch them all the time" (*Neighbours, Home and Away*)
> "*Neighbours* is a different environment, how the other half lives".

Without wishing to make too much of these limited data, it appeared that the offenders in this study were able to and did discriminate between television programmes by the degree to which they felt each programme reflected some broader social reality. They were attracted both to programmes that they felt were 'real' in some sense, and those they clearly felt were not.

Who Would They Choose To Be On Television?

The children were asked a series of questions designed to elicit information about the types of people or characters in the media that they admired or with whom they identified. Thus, for example, they were asked 'If you had the chance to be someone who appears on television, who would you choose to be?' In the main the offenders either did not or felt they could not answer this question. The offenders felt particularly uncomfortable with this question and appeared to have difficulty in understanding why one might want to be such a person. In all, only 27 (39 per cent) of the male offenders identified somebody on television and in only three cases (Arnold Schwarzenegger, Nigel Mansell, and 'a racing driver') was this person identified more than once. Only two of the nine female offenders identified anyone, and on both occasions they were actors in soap operas. Among the sample of schoolchildren, a far higher proportion felt able to answer the question (67 per cent of the boys and 65 per cent of the girls). Arnold Schwarzenegger was most popular among the boys (five per cent) and an actor from Neighbours among the girls (four per cent).

It is interesting to speculate on the reasons for the difficulties encountered by the offenders in choosing to be someone on television. In several interviews, the offenders had already stated that they watched little television, could not remember their favourite programmes and, consequently, could not think of anyone to be. In these cases, their obvious failure to identify with any television characters seemed to be part of a general lack of engagement with television. However, although it was not the subject of this interview, it is also possible that they were less likely to pick television role models than the schoolchildren for other reasons. Further research would be needed to explore these results in the light of a broader understanding of identification with television characters in teenagers.

Video And Cinema Viewing Habits

The children were asked a variety of questions about films they had seen either at the cinema or on video. The questionnaire began by asking them about their use of videos: when had they last watched a video, how often they watched videos from a shop or a club, and how often they used their video recorder to watch programmes recorded earlier off the television. In relation to how recently they had watched a video, the majority of schoolchildren and offenders had seen one or more within the last three days and just less than a third of both groups had seen one within the last 24 hours. The pattern of use of the two groups was in most respects very similar, with the exception that a substantially larger proportion of the offenders had not watched a video within the last month (see Table 3.6).

Table 3.6: How recently the children had watched a video

When they last watched a video	Schoolchildren %	Offenders %
Earlier today/yesterday	30	32
Within the last 3 days	26	27
Within the last week	18	13
Within the last two weeks	9	5
Within the last month	11	4
Longer ago than that	6	19

There were some differences between the two groups of children in the frequency with which they hired films from video shops or clubs. The proportion of offenders who reported renting a video more than once a week was nearly twice that of the schoolchildren. However, by contrast one third of the offenders were very infrequent users of films in this manner hardly ever or never hiring films from a shop or club. This was the case for only 17 per cent of the schoolchildren (see Table 3.7).

Table 3.7: Frequency of video rental

Frequency	Schoolchildren %	Offenders %
More than once a week	15	28
Once a week	17	18
Two to three times a month	24	10
Once a month	13	4
Less than once a month	14	6
Hardly ever/never	17	33

Where the offenders and the schoolchildren departed most significantly was in the extent to which they used the equipment to record programmes from the television. Over half of the schoolchildren said that they watched programmes recorded earlier off the television a minimum of two or three times a week. By contrast the proportion of offenders doing so was less than one fifth and over half of them said that they never did so (see Figure 3.4).

**Figure 3.4: Television time-shift video viewing:
Watching programmes recorded earlier**

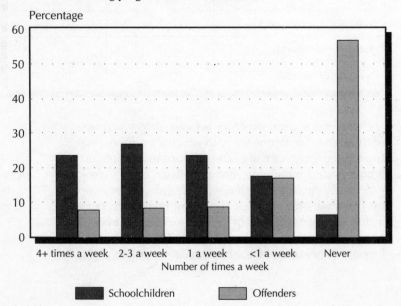

Finally in relation to general media-related behaviour, the offenders and schoolchildren were asked how frequently they went to the cinema. A slightly higher proportion of the offenders said that they visited the cinema frequently, but the differences were marginal. Much more significant was the fact that over half of the offenders said that they rarely or never went to the cinema compared to less than one third of the schoolchildren (see Table 3.8). That said, approximately one third of the offenders said that they went to the cinema at least once a month, a figure similar to the national average for 15-24 year-olds.[5]

Table 3.8: Frequency of cinema attendance

Frequency	Schoolchildren %	Offenders %
More than once a week	1	3
Once a week	4	5
2-3 times per month	17	11
Once a month	22	13
Less than once a month	27	16
Never/rarely	29	52

Video And Cinema Film Preferences

In order to examine the film preferences of these two groups of children, both were asked which films they had seen most recently. Table 3.9 shows the five films seen by the greatest number of schoolchildren and male offenders (the numbers of female young offenders were too small and the range of films they had seen too wide to make it possible to rank the most popular recent films). The project is necessarily a product of its timing. A proportion of the offenders' interviews took place during the early weeks of the release of *Jurassic Park*. Most of the schoolchildren had completed the questionnaires before the release of the film. It is likely that it would have featured higher in the schoolchildren's list a few weeks later. New films and magazines are being released regularly and one of the difficulties of researching in this field is its constantly fluid state.

Table 3.9: Five most recently viewed films
(Film certificate in parentheses.)

Schoolboys	Schoolgirls	Male Offenders
1 Terminator 2 (15)	The Bodyguard (15)	Jurassic Park (PG)
2 Lethal Weapon 3 (15)	Indecent Proposal (15)	Terminator 2 (15)
3 Universal Soldier (18)	Sister Act (PG)	The Bodyguard (15)
4 White Men Can't Jump (15)	Hand That Rocks Cradle (15)	The Cliffhanger (15)
5 Indecent Proposal (15)	Home Alone 1 (PG)	Groundhog Day (PG)

The children were then asked to name their three favourite films - films that they had either seen at the cinema or on video and particularly liked. Perhaps not surprisingly this elicited an enormous list of film titles - more than 600 in all. Drawing firm conclusions therefore from what the children said that they were watching was extremely problematic. There were few films that were identifiably more popular than the rest; indeed the list tended to reflect what had been on release at the cinema within the previous year and what was generally available on video. The top five favourite films of the young male offenders and of the sample of schoolboys is given below in Table 3.10. Unfortunately, given the relatively small number of female offenders in the sample, it is difficult to make general statements about their favourite films and, therefore, the responses of both female offenders and schoolgirls are excluded from the table. Where two certificates are listed for one film, the first is the category granted to the film on general release, the second is the video classification.

One of the major concerns voiced about the viewing habits of young people is the extent to which they have access to, and watch, films with a significant amount of violent imagery. In order to avoid having to make

Table 3.10: Boys Favourite Films
(Film certificates in parentheses.)

	Schoolboys	**Offenders**
1	Terminator 2 (15)	Terminator 2 (15)
2	Point Break (15/18)	New Jack City (18)
3	Aliens (18)	Scarface (18)
4	White Men Can't Jump (15)	The Bodyguard (15)
5	Blood Sport (18)	A.W.O.L. Absent Without Leave (18)

judgements ourselves about which of the films mentioned by the samples in this study might be considered to be especially violent, the titles were distinguished by their film classification[6]. We were thus able to compare the activities of the offenders and the schoolchildren in terms of the extent to which they had recently been watching films with an 18 classification[7], and the extent to which they nominated films with such a classification among their favourites (see Figure 3.5).

Figure 3.5: Certificate of favourite film: Boys only

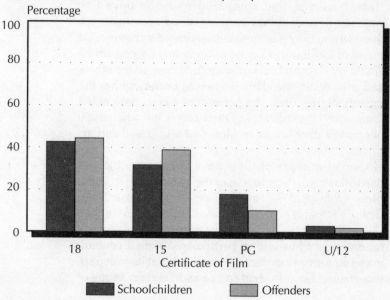

Thus among the male offenders, in answer to a question which asked them to name their three favourite films, they mentioned a total of 62 films of which 28 (45 per cent) had 18 certificates, 25 (40 per cent) 15 certificates, with only a small number having either a PG or 12 certificate (see Figure 3.4). As was suggested above, it was rare for films to be mentioned frequently. Even when titles in a series were taken together this remained the case with, for example, *Terminator 1* and *2* the most popular, being mentioned by seven of the 51 boys answering the question. Very much the same pattern was found among the sample of schoolboys. Once again, films with 18 certificates were mentioned most frequently (44 per cent) with 15 certificates accounting for the majority of the remainder (33 per cent). As was the case with the offenders, the *Terminator* films were, once again, the most popular, being mentioned by 72 boys out of 476. It appears then that the offenders mentioned 18-certificate films with almost identical frequency as the schoolchildren, despite the fact that the mean age of those in the sample of offenders was a little older than that of the schoolchildren.

Once again, given the relatively small number of female offenders in the sample, it is difficult to make general statements about their viewing habits. It was clear, however, that compared with the boys few watched films that had been classified as suitable for those 18 and over. The nine female offenders mentioned a total of 18 films in all of which only one - *Nightmare on Elm Street* - had an 18 classification. Almost all the others had a 15 certificate. This trend was borne out among the schoolgirls, only 11.5 per cent of whom nominated films with 18 certificates as their favourite, whereas 60 per cent of their favourite films had a 15 classification.

A small number of films have been the subject of particular media scrutiny over the last year or so. These films - *Silence of the Lambs, Cape Fear, Reservoir Dogs, Henry: Portrait of a Serial Killer, Bad Lieutenant, Man Bites Dog* and one or two others - have been held up as typical examples of films with a particularly violent content. Such films are also sometimes held to be, at least in part, responsible for supposed increases in certain forms of crime - especially juvenile crime. There is no evidence from the interviews conducted with young offenders and schoolchildren of the same age in this study that these particular films are watched by anything more than a very tiny minority of young people. Of the 69 young male offenders, two claimed to have seen *Cape Fear*, and one mentioned *Reservoir Dogs* and one *Henry: Portrait of a Serial Killer* as being one of their favourite films - none of the other films were mentioned at all. Three other mainstream films about violent criminal lifestyles were chosen as favourites by a few offenders, these were *Mobsters* (chosen by two), *Scarface* (chosen by four), and *Once Upon A Time In America* (chosen by two). Among the schoolboys' favourite films, *Silence of the Lambs* was mentioned 11 times, *Cape Fear* and *Reservoir Dogs* once each, out of a total of 476 boys. None of the nine female offenders mentioned any of these films, whereas two of the 53 schoolgirls mentioned *Silence of the Lambs*. Few hard and fast conclusions can be drawn from such data with the exception that it seems clear that the films most often cited as being 'too violent' and a 'bad influence' appear to be tangential to the lives of most of the young offenders interviewed in this study. It is important to stress the small numbers involved, and the infrequency with which any one film, or indeed type of film, was mentioned. In addition, there were no reports of viewing of unclassified tapes, such as the old 'video nasties', as such titles are virtually absent from any of the lists.

Film Stars and Characters - Identification and Attraction

As was the case in relation to television, the young people in this study were asked questions about which people or characters they identified with in films or who were their favourites. In response to the question 'if you had the chance to be someone who appears in films, who would you choose to be?' a total of 94 alternatives were offered by the 338 schoolchildren answering. Only two actors were nominated by more than ten per cent of the boys: Arnold Schwarzenegger being singled out by 72 boys (21 per cent) and Jean Claude Van Damme by 47 (14 per cent). These two actors remained the top two in the second, third and fourth choices and, therefore, overall. Among the girls, the actors Demi Moore and Julia Roberts were by far the most popular - selected by 17 per cent and 12 per cent of the schoolgirls respectively. The same two actors were the only two people mentioned by young female offenders, though when asked for the names of other people they liked in films they mentioned both Schwarzenegger and Van Damme.

A total of 46 of the male offenders named an actor or character in response to this question. The most popular by far was Arnold Schwarzenegger, who was mentioned by ten of the young offenders. Indeed, among these boys it was the 'macho' stars or characters that dominated their choices (Bruce Willis, Jean Claude Van Damme, Stephen Seagal, Bruce Lee, 'Rambo', Clint Eastwood, 'the hard nut' and 'the person who's not getting shot' were all mentioned). Similarly, when asked to nominate second, third and fourth choices ('Are there any other people in films you particularly like?'), the same actors continued to appear most frequently - a further 14 per cent nominated Schwarzenegger and a similar proportion Jean Claude Van Damme.

Once again, the young offenders' reasons for choosing particular actors or characters were very limited, though in the case of the two most popular choices the same reasons were offered consistently:

"Muscles, action" (Schwarzenegger)
"Muscley (sic), famous" (Schwarzenegger)
"They are all big and muscley (sic)"
(Schwarzenegger, Van Damme, Lundgren)
"Big guy" (Schwarzenegger)
"Brilliant physique and martial arts expert"
(Van Damme)
"Good at karate and all that" (Van Damme)
"Good fighter" (Van Damme)

Machismo in its starkest form - muscles together with an ability to 'handle yourself' - was the thing these boys found most attractive in actors like Schwarzenegger and Van Damme[8]. Rather like their choice of television programmes, however, the word they used most frequently in relation to films and to characters they liked was 'action'. It was clear from the interviews with these children about their lives that many of them spent a significant amount of time feeling bored. It is perhaps not surprising. therefore, that such a high premium is placed on 'action' and 'excitement'.

Computer Games

Finally, the offenders and the schoolchildren were asked about their use of computer games. There appeared to be little difference between the schoolchildren and the offenders in terms of whether or not they played computer or video games. Just over three-quarters of the offenders (77 per cent) and four-fifths of the schoolchildren (81 per cent) said that they did play such games. However, Table 3.11 shows that the locations in which they played differed. Thus, although similar proportions of schoolchildren and offenders played games in arcades, by contrast, and perhaps not surprisingly given the cost of such equipment, a far smaller proportion of offenders than schoolchildren played in their own or a friend's home.

Table 3.11: Frequency of computer game playing by location

Location	Schoolchildren	Offenders
	%	%
In an Arcade	36	39
At Home	81	58
At a Friend's House	51	27

The children were also asked how much time they spent playing computer or video games in a week. Roughly similar proportions of the schoolchildren and the offenders said that they played for less than five hours every week. The difference between the groups came at the top of the range where one in five of the schoolchildren said that they played for over ten hours per week, whereas one in three of the offenders said that they did so (see Figure 3.6). It is possible that part of the explanation for the slightly higher participation in computer games by the offenders arises from the differences in lifestyles between the two groups: many of the offenders were not attending school with the same regularity as the schoolchildren and had more time to fill, as they were not working either.

Figure 3.6: Hours spent playing video games

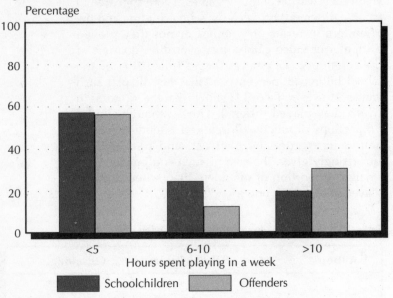

A huge number and variety of computer games were mentioned by the children. Thus, for example, a total of 363 games were mentioned in all, and the 63 male juvenile offenders who answered the question 'what are your (three) favourite games' mentioned a total of 53 different games between them. Not surprisingly, therefore, the preferences expressed were widely spread across the games and it was not the case that a small number of titles were dominant. In addition, a quarter of the offenders and a tenth of the schoolchildren said that they did not play games or had no favourites. That said, Table 3.12 shows those games that were mentioned by the children most frequently. By and large the same games were mentioned by the offenders and the schoolchildren most frequently. In both groups, *Streetfighter* 1 and 2 were the most popular games.

It is difficult to categorise computer games, although in terms of assessing what young children are playing it is clearly important that a system for differentiating between the titles be constructed[9]. A taxonomy used in the Nintendo magazine *Total*[10] divided such games into nine 'types', of which three were basically violent: 'Platform blasters' (such as *Robocop*), 'Beat 'em ups' (such as *Streetfighter*), and "Shoot 'em ups' (such as *Interstellar Assault* and *UN Squadron*). Of the games nominated on most occasions by both the offenders and the schoolchildren - *Streetfighter 1* and *2* were those that would be classified as 'violent', but most of the other four favourite selections (of both groups) were not, and would be classified under the headings of 'sport simulations', 'adventures' or 'platformers'. The exception to this was the joint fifth choice of the offenders, *Mortal Kombat*, which was only mentioned by three out of 78. Although the same names were cropping up in the games most frequently played, a slightly larger proportion of young offenders than schoolchildren played the *Streetfighter* games, which accounted for 23 per cent of the offenders' preferences and 10 per cent of the schoolchildren's.

If such games have any 'effect' on those that play them, it is (as with any other medium) likely to be the way in which they are assimilated by the viewer/player that is of primary importance. Computer games form, by definition, an interactive medium. Given the growth of this industry, and the limited knowledge about how children play and understand such games, this is clearly an area in which further research needs to be conducted.

Table 3.12: Favourite computer games

	Schoolchildren	Offenders
1	Streetfighter 1 & 2	Streetfighter 1 & 2
2	Sonic 1 & 2	Sonic 1 & 2
3	Mario Kart	Supermario
4	Sensible Soccer	Mario
5	Desert Strike Lemmings	Mario Kart Mortal Kombat

Given some of the concerns about the effects of playing computer games[11] the children were asked whether anyone disapproved of their game playing. Once again, the answers from the two groups were comparable, with 22 per cent of each group saying that someone disapproved. Among both the offenders and the schoolchildren it was mainly parents that disapproved. In relation to the offenders, in almost every case the reported reason for disapproval was practical: because it meant that the television could not be used for other purpose, that the noise was annoying or that it was felt to be a waste of time or money. Given the fact that the offenders tended to live in households where having a large number of televisions was unusual, such practical objections should perhaps not be a surprise. Apart from one case in which the offender's mother was apparently concerned about epilepsy, there was no suggestion that playing such games had any harmful consequences for the player. This was not the case among the sample of schoolchildren, who reported a far wider range of objections, almost a quarter of which were linked in some way to health or welfare (bad for eyes; fits; headaches; addiction; tiredness) and a further 28 per cent were because the child was felt to spend too long playing games. Neither the parents of the offenders or the schoolchildren appear to be particularly concerned about the nature or content of the games, and only one child in the study suggested that it was the violence in the games being played that was the reason for disapproval.

Media richness versus media poverty?

Up to this point, uses of various types of media have been treated independently, and no attempt has been made to relate use of one type to use of another. However, it is possible that the overall amount and spread of media usage by offenders and non-offenders might vary, examining all the areas together. Are some respondents 'media rich' and others 'media poor'? Are offenders more or less likely to be media rich than representative schoolchildren?

Each subject was given a score on each of five different measures of media 'engagement' (newspapers, television, films frequency, film character identification, and computer game playing) establishing the level of their engagement with each. Table 3.13 outlines the criteria for achieving a positive score on each different type of media.

Table 3.13: Measuring media richness versus media poverty

Five areas of measurement
Newspaper engagement Reads a newspaper daily
Television engagement Amount of television watched on average weekday is 3 hours or more
Film frequency Watches films from a video shop more than once a month, or goes to the cinema more than once a month
Film character identification Identifies a character in films who they would like to be
Video game engagement Plays video games for more than 5 hours a week.

Each of these sets of criteria, taken separately, led to between one and two thirds of the whole sample of 616 children being identified (44 per cent of the sample had high newspaper involvement, 46 per cent had high television involvement, 57 per cent had high film frequency, 64 per cent had film character identification, and 36 per cent had high game involvement).

The schoolchildren and the offenders were each measured on their overall media engagement by counting up the number of different areas in which each subject scored positively. The lowest score possible was '0', indicating that the subject was in the bottom proportion of the sample for frequency of use of all types of media. The highest score was '5', indicating that the subject was in the top proportion of the sample for frequency of use of all types of media and for access to equipment. Table 3.14 demonstrates that approximately similar numbers of schoolchildren and offenders rated positively both at the bottom and the top end of the 'media rich' scale. Approximately similar proportions had none, one, two, three, four or five areas of high 'media engagement'. A comparison of the average score of "media richness" of the two groups confirms these similarities: the schoolchildren scored an average of 2.5 areas each, the offenders an average of 2.4 areas each.

Table 3.14: Media rich versus media poor: Comparison of schoolchildren and offenders

MEDIA RICH - Number of different areas	Schoolchildren %	Offenders %
No areas	3.0	6.4
One area only	17.3	15.4
Two areas	28.4	26.9
Three areas	27.3	33.3
Four areas	17.3	16.7
Five areas	5.0	1.3

Inevitably, most of the five areas measured - newspaper reading, television viewing, frequency of film viewing, and frequency of game playing - are liable to be affected by household economics. This is likely to be more so for some measurements than for others, but will affect them all to some extent. The similarities between the two groups might be due to the fact that both groups were interested in the written and broadcast media to the same extent or might be due to the possibility that the offenders could not afford to be media rich. It is not clear whether, given the same access to equipment and the same money for cinema attendance or video hire, the offenders might choose to engage more. Further research is needed to establish the influence of socioeconomic status on the viewing habits of young offenders, who will tend to come from fairly deprived backgrounds.

Conclusion

This examination of the reading and viewing habits of a group of young offenders and a comparison group of schoolchildren found that the offenders reported less access to television, video and other equipment than the schoolchildren, and that soap operas and similar dramas dominated the television choices of both groups. Among the offenders *The Bill* was said to be the most popular television programme, whereas *Home and Away* and *Neighbours* were the most popular with schoolboys and schoolgirls respectively, although *The Bill* also featured in the top five television programmes of the schoolboys. The favourite film among both the male offenders and the schoolboys was *Terminator 2*. In general terms the offenders did not report watching more television or select more violent programmes or films than the schoolchildren.

The numbers of titles of television programmes and films reported by both groups was very high. For example, over 600 film titles were mentioned in response to the question concerning favourite films. Although some films were reported more frequently than others, the actual numbers supporting any one choice were always relatively small. Taking the small sample sizes into consideration, such choices can only be treated as qualitatively interesting, rather than as reflecting any statistical validity. The results presented in this chapter only reflect what the children said, not what they actually did. These self-reported viewing data need to be supplemented by further data on viewing behaviour before any firm conclusions can be drawn.

Notes

1. See, for example, Rutter, M. and Giller, H., (1983) *Juvenile Delinquency, Trends and Perspectives*, Harmondsworth: Penguin, or Sturge, C., (1982) 'Reading retardaton and anti-social behaviour', *Journal of Child Psychology and Psychiatry*, 23, 21-31.

2. Gunter, B., McAleer, J. and Clifford, B. (1991) *Children's Views About Television*. Aldershot: Avebury.

3. Research undertaken by the BARB in 1991 found that 85 per cent of homes with both televisions and children had a video recorder. *Cultural Trends 17* (Table 1.25) London: PSI.

4. The small number of female offenders in the sample meant that several programes were nominated the same number of times. The fourth most popular choice for the young female offenders was shared by *Coronation Street, The Bill, Brookside* and *Prisoner Cell Block H.*

5. Directly comparable figures for this age group in general are not available (and the statistics fluctuate quite markedly anyway). The data that do exist, however, suggest that the schoolchildren in this study report slightly higher rates of cinema attendance than might be expected, whereas the offenders' reported rates of cinema attendance are about average. See *Cultural Trends* 17, London: PSI.

6. See Appendix 3 for a description of the BBFC's film classifications and the ages they denote.

7. When this research was carried out, '18' tapes were still clearly accessible to children (the law was tightened up at the end of 1993).

8. Noting such a trend in youth culture more generally, Beatrix Campbell recently commented that 'compelled to quarry for role models only in men, boys saturated by *The Terminator* template make their masculinity in an image that has alienated and exhausted everyone'. "Life without Father. It's easy" *The Independent*, 17 November 1993.

9. In February of this year the Home Office endorsed a Europe-wide scheme for computer games to carry film-style age ratings offering guidelines to purchasers and shop-staff.

10. This is reported in some detail in Griffiths, M. (1993) 'Are computer games bad for children?' *The Psychologist* September, p401-407.

11. See, for example, 'Children Act Out Video Violence', *Daily Telegraph* 25 October 1993, or 'Is your child addicted to computer games?', *The Sun* 18 November 1993 in which it was claimed that 'research shows that more than 60% of boys and 30% of girls aged 13 to 15 are addicted'.

Chapter 4 **Viewing habits of violent juvenile offenders**

Background

The bulk of juvenile offending is not violent. Violent offences generally form less than ten per cent of recorded juvenile crime. The majority of juvenile crime is made up of various kinds of theft, burglary, road traffic offences and damage to property[1]. In addition, research conducted by PSI suggests that juvenile offenders do not appear to specialise in particular sorts of offending, and frequent offenders who do have a violent offence on their record will often have committed a range of other types of non-violent offence as well, such as driving without insurance or shop theft. The fact that most juvenile offenders are not violent is frequently overlooked by commentators in the media. In addition, in speculating on the possible effects of certain types of programmes and films, there is often a failure to distinguish offenders who are frequently in trouble from those who have committed very serious offences but who may have done so infrequently. Frequency should not be confused with seriousness. Whilst offences of violence represent approximately one tenth of juvenile offences, the most serious such as murder or attempted murder, rape and other serious sexual assaults are far rarer.

Nonetheless, despite the relative rarity of acts of major violence by teenage offenders, concerns that the regular viewing of violent acts may be associated with violent offending are often expressed both by members of the public and by organisations involved in television and broadcasting. This chapter will address this issue by looking specifically at the viewing habits and preferences of offenders who have at least one conviction for violent crime. It is worth reiterating at this stage that this is an exploratory study designed to examine viewing habits and preferences and not as a piece of research that could or would consider the meaning and implication of associations (or the lack of associations) between such habits and preferences and offending behaviour. The question of media influences on the behaviour of young offenders will have to be left to larger-scale, more sophisticated studies. A number of other caveats need to be entered at this point. First, this study focuses on a small, though nevertheless interesting, group of juvenile offenders. Consequently, drawing general conclusions from the data needs to be undertaken with great care. Sub-dividing the sample in order to focus on offenders with convictions for violence further limits the numbers and increases the caution that must be taken when drawing inferences from the data.

Of the 78 interviewed offenders, police records identified 30 who had, among their other crimes, a caution or a conviction in 1992 for some kind of violent offence (violence against the person). Four of these offenders were girls. The violent offences included grievous bodily harm ('GBH', which implies physical harm to the victim including broken bones, severe cuts, bruising, etc), actual bodily harm (ABH, where harm can include less serious cuts and bruises), and robbery (taking something from someone using threatening behaviour or violence, ie, 'mugging'). There is little doubt that any definition of an 'offence of violence' would include these categories. Between them, the convictions attributed to these 30 young people included one count of GBH, 39 counts of ABH and 22 robberies in the course of one year (out of over 500 offences in total). In addition to these three offence types, other offences such as aggravated burglary and aggravated car theft may involve some violence and among the 78 there were offenders who had been successfully prosecuted for such offences. The extent of violence in such cases is less easy to judge, however, and therefore the analyses presented here are based only on young people who had committed the offences of GBH, ABH and robbery. There were no recorded convictions for murder, manslaughter, rape or other serious sexual offences among the sample. In order to assess the viewing habits of these 30 offenders, their answers to questions concerning their viewing preferences were isolated from offenders who had not been convicted of specifically violent offences in 1992.

An examination of the records of the first three offenders on this list of 30 (randomly ordered) illustrates the point that a variety of offences rather than some form of specialisation was the norm. The first was interviewed in a local authority secure unit. He was thirteen, and had committed offences of shoplifting, carrying an offensive weapon (the police record said this was a "rice flail"), criminal damage and robbery in 1992. The second was also thirteen, and had cases of attempted robbery, ABH, suspected theft of a moped and theft from a taxi on his record. The third was fifteen. He had six offences on his record in 1992, including driving without insurance, driving without a licence, criminal damage, theft, assault and robbery. The robbery was valued at over £3,000.

Violent offenders' reading preferences

Two thirds of this group reported that they did not read magazines or comics, and one third did not read newspapers. Of the limited range of magazines that they enjoyed, only two received the votes of three offenders, these were *Smash Hits* and *Beano*. The remainder included *The Dandy*, *TV Times*, *Viz* and *Football Monthly*. If they reported that they did read a newspaper, this was overwhelmingly *The Sun* or the local evening paper.

Violent offenders' favourite television programmes

The 30 offenders with records for violence listed the same set of television programmes as the group as a whole had done. Table 4.1 shows the most popular five programmes, together with the numbers of offenders who mentioned each programme among their choices.

Table 4.1: Violent offenders' favourite television programmes

Favourite programmes	Number of violent offenders mentioning each programme
The Bill	16
Home and Away	11
Neighbours	10
Eastenders	9
Prisoner Cell Block H	5
Did not have favourites	8

Once again, top of their list was *The Bill*, mentioned by over half of them as one of their top five programmes. The remaining four most popular programmes were *Home and Away, Neighbours, Eastenders* and *Prisoner Cell Block H*. Again, it is worth pointing out that the schoolchildren also identified *The Bill* amongst their favourites, but it did not rank as highly in their preferences.

Only seven of the violent offenders had been able to name five programmes; eight had been unable to name any favourites at all. They demonstrated even more difficulty in naming anyone they would like to be on television; only eight children replied with anything other than 'No one' or 'Don't know'. There were no duplicates in their list. The only two people mentioned specifically by name were 'Eddie Murphy', and 'Bruce Lee'. Two offenders suggested roles in *Home and Away*. The remainder included 'Somebody rich', 'A racing driver', 'Kim Basinger's husband', and finally, 'a presenter on Crimewatch UK'.

Violent offenders' favourite films

When asked to name their three favourite films, only a half of the violent offenders named as many as three favourites. Five of the 30 violent offenders could not name any favourite films. Of those who had favourites, these followed the general trend for the rest of the offenders and the schoolchildren in reflecting a wide range of films on release in the cinema and on video (a total of 42 titles) and there was little consensus amongst them. Because of the spread of choices, the list reveals little in the way of patterns among the violent offenders' viewing preferences. However, given the level of general interest expressed in these types of data, all forty-two titles are listed in Table 4.2, together with the number of offenders viewing each.

Table 4.2: Violent offenders' favourite films
(number of offenders mentioning each title in parentheses)

Beverley Hills Cop (2)	Juice (1)
The Bodyguard (2)	The Last Action Hero (1)
Boyz n the Hood (2)	The Lost Boys (1)
Child's Play (3)	Me, You and Myrtle (1)
The Chuka Master (1)	Mobsters (1)
Cocktail (1)	The Nasty Boys (1)
Coming to America (1)	New Jack City (3)
Die Hard (3)	Nightmare on Elm Street (1)
Dogs in Space (1)	Once Upon a Time in America (2)
Enemy Mine (1)	Predator (1)
Fantasia (1)	Pretty Woman (1)
A Few Good Men (1)	Robin Hood: Prince of Thieves (1)
Flowers in the Attic (1)	Scarface (1)
Full Metal Jacket (1)	Terminator 2 (3)
Game of Death II (1)	The Colour Purple (1)
Ghost (2)	Too Young to Die (1)
Grease (1)	Total Recall (1)
Henry, Portrait of a Serial Killer (1)	Turk Horse (1)
The Hidden (1)	White Men Can't Jump (1)
Home Alone 2 (2)	Who will love my children (1)
Indecent Proposal (1)	Ultimate Rave (1)

Few offenders identified the same films. Only four films were identified by as many as three offenders; these were *Terminator 2*, *Child's Play*, *Die Hard* and *New Jack City*. Given the range of films on offer to young people, the range reflected in their choice is not surprising. However, the list demonstrates that not only did different offenders select different titles as their favourites, they also appeared to favour quite different genres, their selections ranging from *Grease* and *Fantasia*, through *Indecent Proposal to Scarface*. No obvious patterns of preference emerge.

Offenders were asked to report how many times they had viewed their favourite film, and in order to assess whether there was any particular obsession with certain films, all films that any offender reported they had viewed ten times or more were listed. This list again reflected a range of film types and certificates, and all films reportedly viewed ten times or more by any violent offender are listed in Table 4.3.

Table 4.3: Films viewed repeatedly by violent offenders
(Number of times reportedly viewed by any one offender in parentheses)

Beverley Hills Cop (11)
The Chuka Master ("loads")
Cocktail (50+)
Die Hard (25)
Dogs in Space (30)
Enemy Mine ("over 100")
Fantasia ("loads")
Full Metal Jacket (30)
Game of Death 2 ("loads")
Grease ("loads")
The Lost Boys ("over 100")
Predator (30)
Pretty Woman (20)
Scarface ("lots")
Terminator 2 (two offenders 10/15)
The Colour Purple (15)
Total Recall (15)
Ultimate Rave ("lots")
White Men Can't Jump (12)

The first thing to note from this list is that it is obviously not a wholly reliable research strategy to ask young people to say how many times they have seen a film. The number of offenders who claimed to have watched a film "loads", "lots" or "over 100" times suggests that they had at best only a rough idea of how often they had seen them. Where offenders did state a number, it is quite probably not reliably different from say 15, 20, or any other quite high response. Interviewees' responses to this question concerning their favourite films are probably best viewed as an indication that they *liked* these films, and had seen them *repeatedly*, but it is doubtful that much more than this can be read into the data. Only one film had been frequently viewed by two offenders, and this was *Terminator 2*, violent perhaps, but undoubtedly mainstream. Again, the choices reflect a variety of genres, including some especially violent films such as *Scarface*, but equally, including some strikingly non-violent films such as *Cocktail, Grease,* and *Fantasia.*

Conclusion

The lack of consensus amongst the full group of juvenile offenders was reflected in the sub-group of offenders cautioned or convicted of violent offences in 1992. There were no generalisable statements that could be made concerning the preferences of the 'violent' group when compared to the rest of the offenders, or to the schoolchildren. Where it was possible for the violent offenders to think of a favourite television programme or film, they tended to name a range of titles that were very similar if not identical to those named by the remainder of the children in the study. No one particular film proved overly popular with this group, and films that they liked to view again and again included romances and fantasy as well as mainstream "macho" action films. It is worth reporting that of the schoolchildren, two reported multiple viewing of each of the following films: *Aliens, Bloodsport, Kickboxer* and *Silence of the Lambs*, amongst others.

What this and the previous chapter illustrate is that untangling viewing preferences is complicated, and requires careful and rigorous attention, beyond the scope of this project. The methodological limitations of interviewing teenagers about their memories of programmes and films seen are highlighted by their answers, particularly in response to the request to estimate how many times they had seen particular films. Before even reaching a situation where the *influence* of viewing preferences on offending behaviour might begin to be tackled, more sophisticated work has to be done on establishing what it is that violent children like about particular programmes and films. In order to address this issue directly, attention might more profitably be directed at serious offenders, rather than at frequent offenders.

Notes
1. See *Criminal Statistics England and Wales*, HMSO, published annually.

Chapter 5   Social and family context of offenders' media use

The previous chapters have outlined the viewing behaviours and choices of the two samples, and this exercise has not yet suggested any clear differences between the two groups. The offenders chose to watch much the same kinds of material as the schoolchildren, although they ranked one or two television programmes, *The Bill* in particular, more highly than the schoolchildren. They appeared to watch approximately similar amounts of television, although they may have been more likely to do some of their viewing later at night. Findings such as this latter raise the question of alternative or different patterns in the social and family context of media use by offenders. Where were the offenders seeing their programmes and films? Who were they viewing with? Against what sort of household arrangements was viewing taking place? Background information was not collected on the sample of schoolchildren and, consequently, much of this chapter only relates to the offenders. It was possible, however, to ask both groups where and with whom they were doing their viewing, and this is considered below.

Living circumstances of offenders

One of the first points to note from Chapter 2 above, in relation to the living circumstances of the offenders, was that a small minority of them were not living at home, but in some sort of custodial or alternative provision such as Young Offenders Institutions, Local Authority secure accommodation or children's homes (approximately 17 per cent in total). To differing extents, each of these will influence their access to television, video and film. In fact, it appeared that there was always access to viewing at some point in the day, but the timing may have been restricted, and, depending on the number of other people in the wing or unit, control over what was watched varied considerably. Wherever possible, if offenders were in custody at the time of the interview, questioning was directed at their experiences outside, but in cases where they had been in custody for several months recall of previous situations was likely to be variable. Of those offenders not in custody (and only a minority were), approximately a third (31%) were living at home with both their parents. The remainder were either with one parent or a grandparent (46% in total), or were living elsewhere, neither with families nor in custody (six per cent).

A second point to note is that the offenders came from distinctly disadvantaged backgrounds in comparison to what might be expected for representative schoolchildren. A substantial proportion of the heads of their households were unemployed or out of work due to child care demands or sickness. In these viewing data, the only reflection of the nature of their backgrounds in comparison to representative children lay in their accounts of availability of viewing equipment: numbers of televisions in the household, having their own television in their rooms, and access to satellite and cable. From the interview contacts, it was obvious that lack of material wealth, contact with social welfare agencies, and other indicators of disadvantage were over-represented in this group of adolescents.

For those offenders living at home or independently, the overriding impression gained in the interviewing was of lives that were full of change and chaos. This was reflected, in part, by the low response rate to the interviewing approach, as many were untraceable or uncontactable. Many offenders, if not currently in the care of the prison service or the local authority, will, at some point in their lives, have lived somewhere other than in the family home. One possible consequence of this is that media habits are likely to be subject to changing backgrounds as the offender moves between different contexts.

As well as these household changes, a substantial proportion of the offenders interviewed were living a quite different lifestyle to the schoolchildren. This was most obviously evidenced in the fact that over half said they had permanently left school by the time of the interview (59%), including eight of those who were under 16 at the time of the interview. By definition, of course, all of the schoolchildren were still attending school. The groups were approximately matched for age, so this difference is not likely to be entirely a function of the offenders being slightly older. Only a fifth of the offenders were actually attending school at the time of the interview, which took place towards the end of the summer term or in the summer holiday. Of those who had left school, over half were unemployed. The remainder were involved in part-time or full- time work, or were at home but not actively seeking work. These factors will necessarily affect their viewing habits.

Offenders were interviewed in a range of situations where building up regular television and film viewing habits might be assumed to be difficult. One, for example, was living in a caravan, others in friends' houses. One who responded that he had a television in his bedroom was actually sleeping in the living room. Many had run away from home at some point in their lives. In one case, the child had lived on the streets for over three months, some while before the interview took place.

Such comments can only serve an illustrative and indicative purpose. However, they indicate the need to consider the broader context in which viewing occurs, and despite similarities in final choice of viewing, the background against which this takes place is likely to be very different for young offenders than for representative schoolchildren.

Where were films being viewed?

Both groups were asked to indicate where each of their five most frequently viewed films had been seen. Unfortunately, given the differences in the administration of the question - as a questionnaire item for schoolchildren, as an interview question for offenders, the responses are not directly comparable.

Thus, the schoolchildren were given two choices, on video or at the cinema. The offenders had rather more freedom in their responses, and could list a wider range of options, including 'on television'. However, bearing in mind these methodological differences, the responses of the two groups are interesting to compare. The schoolchildren reported between them a total of 2081 recent viewings of films, nearly four each. Three quarters of these were reported to have been viewed on video, the remaining quarter at the cinema. In over 100 cases, they could not remember or did not answer the question.

For the 78 offenders, who had a total of 209 individual viewings between them, rather fewer than three each, half had taken place on video, and a quarter at the cinema. The remainder had been viewed on television, or the response given had not fitted any of these categories. These additional responses included viewing in custody, where the offender could not always distinguish between films broadcast on television or replayed on video.

Thus, similar numbers of most recent film viewings had reportedly taken place at the cinema. This result was slightly surprising; given the lower rates of access to equipment in their households, it had been anticipated that there would also be less money for cinema attendance in the group of offenders. Fewer of the offenders than the schoolchildren reported viewing their most recent film on video but this might partly be due to the fact that they had the option to say it had been viewed on television. As the schoolchildren were not given this option, it is possible that they were either ignoring films seen on TV when giving their most recent five, or were squashing those seen on television into the 'video' category.

Who were films being viewed with?

For each of their most recently viewed films, the two groups were asked to identify with whom they saw the film. Again, there were methodological differences in the way in which this question was presented, relating to the differences between interview and questionnaire administration. The offenders had a choice of six different types of company: 'Friends', 'Parents', 'Other family', 'Adults (non-family)', 'Alone' and a "catch-all" final category of 'Others (non-adult)'. The final category was used by some offenders to reflect other inmates in the YOI or other residents in the children's home, neither of whom would be considered 'Friends'. In addition, it transpired that they preferred to place girlfriends and boyfriends in this 'Other' category; people who they did not consider should fall in the 'Friends' category. The schoolchildren were only given five categories, which included Friends, Parents, Other family, Adults and Alone, but which excluded the final 'Other' category. These methodological differences make it slightly awkward to compare the rankings of the two groups in terms of the viewing company they were keeping. However, the results to this question are shown in Table 5.1. Where the respondents identified two or more categories of company (which occurred in approximately ten per cent of cases) both are included in this list.

Table 5.1: **Rankings of company for most recently viewed films**

Rank	Schoolchildren (out of five choices)	Offenders (out of six choices)
1	Friends	Friends
2	Alone	Others (non-adult)
3	Parents	Other family (non-adult)
4	Other family (non-adult)	Parents
5	Adults (non-family)	Alone
6	–	Adults (non-family)

Both groups reported overwhelmingly that they had watched their most recently viewed films with their friends. For the offenders this represented 56 per cent of their viewings, for the schoolchildren it represented 54 per cent. The differences arose in the categories ranking second and third after 'friends'. For the schoolchildren, the categories of company ranked second and third were alone, or with their parents. For the offenders, second rank of company was, unexpectedly, the "catch-all" 'Other' category. The offenders' third ranking of company was other, non-parental family members. The non-parental family members were usually siblings.

Of course, it remains unknown whether or not the schoolchildren would have made as much use of the 'Other' category as did the offenders. However, even excluding this category from the comparisons, it appeared that the offenders were less likely to be viewing films alone, and more likely to be viewing with other (non-adult) members of their family. 'Alone' was ranked second from the top by the schoolchildren, but second from last by the offenders. These results may well reflect the lower socio- economic status of the offenders, whose living conditions were perhaps more likely to be cramped than those of their representative peers, many more of whom had televisions in their own rooms. As a result, the offenders may have been less able to opt to watch programmes and films on their own, and, consequently, one might infer that they were less likely to have complete control over what they were watching, as the viewing preferences of others (brother, sisters, other residents, other inmates) would have influenced the viewing sessions.

Conclusion

This discussion has raised the possibility that one reason for the tendency for the offenders to name fewer favourite television programmes, fewer favourite films and to identify fewer people they would like to be on the screen may be due in part to a background and lifestyle less conducive to building up strong attachments to set viewing patterns than that of other, less offending, samples. The following chapter expands and illustrates some of the main themes suggested above by presenting a series of thirteen case studies of the viewing habits of the most frequent offenders in 1992.

Chapter 6   Case studies of 13 most frequent offenders

Introduction

Figure 2.1 in Chapter 2 identified thirteen offenders who all had over twenty known and alleged offences recorded on their police files within the previous year. Particular media attention is focused on the viewing habits of the most frequent young offenders, and, in order to look at these in more detail, brief individual case descriptions were drawn up for all thirteen. However, it should be noted that these offenders were identified on the basis of one type of official offending only ('known and alleged'). Frequency of offending can be measured in a number of different ways and over various different time scales[1]. For example, juveniles will not be arrested for all offences, and self-reported offending may give a different picture of who is offending most frequently. In addition, police action (and reaction) will vary in different areas and with different individuals or families, and some children in families where there are already known offenders may be more likely to come to the attention of the police and consequently be arrested more frequently. For these reasons, these case studies should be treated as illustrative of *some* of the most frequent offenders in this group. There will be others in the group, perhaps better able to escape police attention, who were offending as frequently but who were not caught as often.

These case studies include seven children who featured in Chapter Four, as members of the 30 offenders who had violent convictions. As this chapter will demonstrate, distinguishing between them on the basis of their official offending is not particularly meaningful, as many admit to a range of offences for which they were not prosecuted. On average, this group of 13 offenders had 32 known or alleged offences for 1992 on their police files, including offences taken into consideration in court. They are all boys. They are fairly evenly spread across the age range, from one who was eleven at the start of 1992 to two who were sixteen at that time. All names and some details have been changed to preserve anonymity.

Case 1

Background: Jim was interviewed in a Local Authority secure unit, where he had been for two months. Before this placement, he said that he had been in another children's home for three months. He had just turned thirteen at the time of the interview, and had experienced four other separate placements by social services in the year prior to the interview. He was on the Local Authority child protection register. Before these placements, he had lived with his parents. His mother was unemployed, and his father worked in a plastics factory. He was under a social services supervision order. He was not attending school, and was not interested in having anything to do with it. He had truanted, up to a term in the previous year when he was still attending school. He had fought at school, for which he was suspended, and hangs around with a group of children from the various children's homes in the area, with whom he gets arrested. At times, he claimed, his weekly spending money reaches £200.

He does not drink at the moment, but has drunk in the past, although not heavily. His drug use is varied, and has included marijuana, amphetamines, hallucinogens, ecstasy, glue sniffing, crack, and sniffing petrol. He has been referred to a psychiatrist as part of a court order.

The interview started reasonably passively, but as it progressed Jim became distracted and fairly destructive, pulling putty out of window frames, tearing pictures off the wall, and ripping his trainers up. At the same time, another child was throwing a tantrum across the hallway, kicking windows and screaming. Throughout all this Jim remained friendly to the interviewer, who commented 'Although he was quite small, he obviously liked to play the hard boy, but on the occasions he smiled he still seemed very young'.

Offending: Jim had 25 known or alleged offences on his police file, including many for criminal damage, actual bodily harm (including one case brought by a police woman), burglary (from a school), robbery (of shoes), theft from a shop, one count of grievous bodily harm, several car offences, and one count of setting off the fire alarm in an old people's home.

By his own report, he was very actively involved in offending, and his account corroborated the police record. It included stealing from cars, people and shops, burglary, and threatening people with weapons. He also added buying and selling stolen goods, fighting in public, buying and selling drugs, drunk driving, and arson. He enjoys driving and, although he appreciated that driving without a licence or insurance in a stolen car were offences and might even result in someone getting killed, he believed that this would not happen to him because his driving was very good. The 'thieving' he does for the money, not enjoyment. The fighting is something that just happens, 'it happens quite a lot to me though'.

Media and viewing habits: Jim's favourite reading was *The Beano* and *The Dandy*, followed by Sega magazines, *Viz* and *Acne*. He reads the cartoons in newspapers. There were televisions in the secure unit, but he does not have one in his bedroom. Videos, radios and stereo systems are also available. He watches a minimum of six hours television a day, from the morning until 11pm at night, and his favourite programme is *The Bill*. Beyond this he has no preferences, simply watching 'anything that comes on'. When asked what it was he enjoyed about *The Bill*, he simply responded 'Its good, I like it, so I watch it', a fairly common type of response. Despite the high level of his television viewing, there was no one who he would want to be on television, and when asked who his favourite people were, he also denied that there was anyone, 'I've got no favourite people'.

Jim watches prerecorded videos approximately once a week, but never uses a video recorder to watch programmes recorded at other times. He didn't know how often he went to the cinema, he simply couldn't answer the question. Similarly, he couldn't answer the question concerning the five most recently viewed films. He could not remember, and thus could not supply details concerning who he was viewing them with. This is despite the fact that his regular television viewing must encompass many films and he had probably viewed five in the week prior to the interview. In response to further prompting, he denied that he had any favourite films at all. He did say that he was allowed to watch 15 and 18 certificate films in the children's home, but again, couldn't name any or think of anyone in films who he would want to be and had no favourite people in films.

He plays video games (on a Sega Mega Drive) in the secure unit, for approximately 15-20 hours a week, but he just tends to play whatever is on offer and, predictably by this point, had no favourites. When asked if there was anyone in the world who he would like to be, he answered, no, just himself.

Case 2

Background: Bob was seventeen at the time of the interview, and was interviewed in a Young Offenders Institution (YOI), where he had been for one month. Prior to this, he had been living at a friend's house for a couple of months, and before that with his parents, on and off. His mother worked in a bar, and his father was unemployed. His relationship with his parents was reasonable by his account, although he reported that he had just received a letter from his father saying that he did not want him to return home again. He had run away from home several times, and had spent time in children's homes. He had left school, and in the previous year he had missed over one term. Prior to being sentenced to custody, his weekly spending had been approximately £600. His drinking (prior to custody) was heavy; over 40 units a week. His drug use included marijuana, amphetamines, hallucinogens, glue sniffing and cocaine. He had been seen by a psychologist for his offending behaviour. Bob was chatty, smartly dressed, and bright.

Offending: By his own account, Bob had committed 25 burglaries in the month just prior to custody, together with 30 occasions of driving without a licence or insurance, two counts of drunk driving, ten counts of stealing from people, and he regularly bought and sold stolen goods. He buys drugs once a month, although he does not sell. Violence was rarer, and (unusually for these children) he did not carry a weapon, although he did admit to having injured someone. Bob's official record contained 59 offences committed in 1992 and known to the police. Thirty-five of these had been taken into consideration. The official record also suggested little violence.

Media and viewing habits: Bob did not read anything, neither comics nor newspapers. In his friend's home, where he had been before custody, he had had access to one communal television and also had a television in his room. There had also been a video recorder but no satellite or cable access. In the YOI he watched television occasionally, in the morning and the early evening, but reported less than one hour a day in total and also said that this was more than he would have viewed prior to custody. He had no favourite programmes, said that there was no one who he would want to be on television, and that he had no favourite people, all due to the fact that he watched so little.

He had watched a video earlier in the day prior to the interview, and at home he used to see approximately one a week. He never used a video recorder to tape programmes himself. Cinema attendance was relatively high, as he reported going more than once a week when not in custody. Most recently he could report details of four films all seen at the cinema with friends; *Predator II*, which he saw between 9pm and 11pm, *Terminator 2*, viewed before 1pm (according to him, although it seems unlikely), *That's my Girl*, seen in the evening, and *Cliffhanger*, seen earlier in the day. His three favourite films were *Double Impact* (seen at the cinema, twice), *Terminator 2* (at the cinema, once) and *A.W.O.L. Absent Without Leave* (at the cinema, three times).

If he could choose to be anyone in films, Bob would be Rambo, because 'He does mad things, and he is a good actor'. He also liked Jean Claude Van Damme, "because of the fighting, and because he is a good actor, and his films have good story lines". Bob rarely played video games and could not name any. These would be played in an arcade.

Case 3

Background: Mark was 15 at the time of the interview, living with his mother, sister and brother and attending school. He had spent time in a children's home. His mother was not working and he had no contact with any father figure. He first ran away from home when he was 10, and was under a supervision order at the time of the interview. He liked school, reported that he had been told his schoolwork was good, but had been permanently excluded from a previous school for truancy. In the year prior to interview he had missed more than one full term. He has just the one friend, a 25 year old man who lives across the road, who Mark described as 'backward'.

The interview was very pleasant, Mark was very amicable, cooperative and interesting. 'The house', wrote the interviewer, 'was the closest I've ever seen to resembling the after effects of an H-bomb'. The interviewer also commented that despite the one friend, Mark obviously mixed with a lot of other people in his drug sessions. He drinks approximately 60 units a week, and uses a range of drugs including marijuana every day, barbiturates, amphetamines, hallucinogens, and a clinical anaesthetic recently new to the teenage drug scene.

Offending: By his own account, Mark's offending was very heavy. In the month leading up to the interview, he had illegally driven cars, stolen from shops, stolen from cars, bought stolen goods, carried weapons, bought and sold drugs, and injured someone. His official record for the previous year contained 22 offences, including extracting electricity, burglaries, cashing a stolen giro book, theft of milk, and theft from a supermarket. He had also fired an airgun, and stolen a bicycle.

Media and viewing habits: Mark could only name three magazines or comics that he read regularly, and these were *Archimedos User, Bike* and *Indy-Car Special.* He read *The Daily Star* newspaper every day. There were three televisions in the house, but none in his bedroom. There was also a video-recorder, but no access to satellite or cable. He watched a great deal of television; over six hours every day, during every time period of the day including 11pm-6.30am. He could only name four favourite television programmes. The first of these was *Prisoner Cell Block H,* followed by *Nigel Mansell's Indy Car, Roseanne* and *Cheers.* The first of these was enjoyed for 'the things that happen in it', including the violence, killing and stealing. The car programme was enjoyed simply because of the racing. If Mark could be anyone on television, it would be a racing driver. His other favourite people on television are Roseanne Arnold and the whole cast of her programme, because of the 'laughs', and the fact that they are "sarcastic to each other".

Mark rarely watches videos, and very occasionally records programmes off the television (less than once a week). These programmes will simply be things that were on while he was doing something else. He hardly ever goes to the cinema. He could only name four films seen recently (rather than the five requested), all of which were viewed on a video. These were *Predator II, Terminator 2, Beverley Hills Cop* and *Dune.* The first three were viewed alone, the last with his family. The first three he claimed to have seen many times, the last over 100 times. At his most recent viewing of these films, he saw the first three between 1pm and 6pm, the last later in the evening. His three favourite films are *Dogs in Space, The Lost Boys,* and *Enemy Mine.* Again, all three were viewed on video, and he claimed to have seen the first thirty times, and the last two over 100 times. If he could be anyone in films, Mark would be Jason Patrick in *The Lost Boys,* because he likes vampires and he believes Jason's to be 'a good character' (interesting rather than moral). Other people who he likes are the lead in *Dune,* although Mark couldn't remember his name, and Eddie Murphy. Reasons? Just because he likes the scripts.

Mark plays computer games, at an arcade, for approximately 10-15 hours a week. His favourite games are *Sonic II, Thunderblade, Hard Driving,* and *Superbowl*. If he could be anybody in the world, he would still be himself.

Case 4

Background: John was fourteen at the time of the interview, living with his father and brother, where he had been for a year and a half. Both his mother and father were unemployed. He had spent time in various different children's homes, and had lived on the streets for three and a half months at one point in his recent past. He was on the Local Authority child protection register. Although he likes school, and hopes to be a car mechanic, he truants regularly, and missed more than one term in the year prior to the interview.

Offending behaviour: By his account, John's offending had included burglary, criminal damage, shop theft, car theft, robbery, selling stolen cheque books, arson and injury. However, he had not offended in the month leading up to the interview. His official record for 1992 included fifteen known offences, ranging from theft from shops, through ABH to criminal damage. He had one official case of arson, three burglaries, several pending cases, and at least five offences taken into consideration by a court.

Media and viewing habits: John reads a newspaper (*Today*) every day, but nothing else. There are two television sets in the house, but none in his bedroom. The house had a video, but no satellite or cable. He watches approximately 2-3 hours on a weekday, rather more on Saturdays, and none on Sundays. His favourite television programme is *The Bill*, followed by *Coronation Street, Prisoner Cell Block H, Eastenders* and *Neighbours*. *The Bill* was considered to be 'real', the others 'good'. Given the choice, he would not be anyone on television, and he had no favourite people. His father disapproved of him watching the soaps.

He saw a video within the 24 hours before the interview, and watches videos from shops approximately once a week. He uses the video two or three times a week to record films, which he plays back at other times. He rarely, if ever, goes to the cinema. He could only name four films seen recently, and these were *Made in America, Jurassic Park, Beverly Hills Cop* and *Lethal Weapon*. The first two were seen at the cinema (despite the fact that he had just said he rarely went), the second two on video. The first and third were seen in the early evening, and the second and last in the afternoon. The first two were seen with friends, *Beverly Hills Cop* was viewed alone, and *Lethal Weapon* seen with a parent. All except the third had only been viewed three times. He named his two favourite films (he didn't have a third) as being *Coming to America* and *Beverley Hills Cop II*. Both of these were seen on video, the first just once, the second eleven times.

If John could be anyone on television, it would be Eddie Murphy, because he's funny. He also likes Whoopi Goldberg for the same reason, and Sean Connery because he makes good films. He couldn't name any others. He plays video games, at home, for up to five hours a week. His favourite games are *Alex Kid, After Burner*, and *Streetfighter*. If he could be anyone in the world, he'd be Eddie Murphy. 'He's my star'.

Case 5

Background: Anthony was seventeen at interview, and he had been unemployed for a month. Prior to this he had been in decorating. He lived with his mother and step-father, and (unusually) he had lived at home all of his life. Both of his parents were working. He had truanted heavily from school before leaving, and had been suspended for setting off fire alarms during examinations. He had been in the army cadets. His friends disapprove of him 'going places they don't want to go'. He drinks approximately 15 units a week, but does not use any drugs. His mother had sought psychological help for him through a family therapy group. Anthony (and his mother) enjoyed the interview, which involved much laughter. 'Not much of a villain', wrote the interviewer, '...obviously quite close to his Mum.'

Offending: Anthony had relatively low levels of self-reported offending, and in the last month the only thing he admitted to was getting into 18 certificate films by lying about his age. Apart from this, the only other offences he had ever committed, he said, were carrying weapons, using them to threaten people, and getting into fights. However, his official record for the previous year contained 32 offences, mostly for theft (of army equipment, milk, sandwiches and a tracksuit), threatening behaviour, burglary and carrying a six inch knife.

Media and viewing habits: Apart from looking at the newspaper to see what was on television (*The Daily Mirror*), Anthony did not use written media. There were three televisions in the house, one of which was in his bedroom. They had a video and also cable television, although he did not have any of the movie channels. He watched between 5-6 hours of television on an average weekday, but less than an hour at the weekends. He could only name two favourite television programmes, these were *The Bill*, and *Soldier Soldier*. The first was 'just all right to watch,' but his interest in the second stemmed from a desire to join the army. There was no one on television who he would like to be, and he had no favourite people. He watches videos, but gets few from video shops. He records from the television himself, and again his interest in the military dictated his choice - *Soldier Soldier*, anything military, and action films. He rarely goes to the cinema. The five films he saw most recently were *Double Impact* (seen once), *Home Alone* (seen 30 times), *Terminator* (seen 100 times, but he didn't say which version), *Full Metal Jacket* (seen 30 times) and *Operation Petticoat* (seen ten times). On the most recent occasions, all of these were seen on the video at his home, the first two with friends, *Terminator* with his parents, *Full Metal Jacket* alone, and the last with his girlfriend.

His three favourite films were *Terminator 2*, *Full Metal Jacket* and *Predator*. The first two have been covered, the third was seen on video, thirty times. If he could be anyone on television, it would be (predictably) Arnold Schwarzenegger, because 'he's just right for the stuff he does'. He also likes Jean Claude Van Damme, 'just because I enjoy his films'.

He plays video games, at a friend's house, on a SEGA Mega Drive, for up to five hours a week. He particularly likes *Streetfighter, Desert Strike* and *Terminator*. There is no one in the world he would prefer to be.

Case 6

Background: Matt was seen in a YOI, where he had been for a month. He was a week past his seventeenth birthday at the interview. Previously he had lived at his family home. Neither of his parents were working. He had left school in the fourth year and said he had not been pursued by the Local Authority. Prior to this he had been suspended for setting off fire alarms. He believed that he had got into trouble because he was in with the 'wrong crowd', and needed money. He doesn't drink, but he does use drugs, including marijuana, amphetamines, hallucinogens, and glue sniffing. Matt was not engaged in the interview, and was mainly taking part in order to get out of work at the YOI, so he was not particularly chatty.

Offending: By his own report, Matt had stayed clear of illegal driving, although he had actually stolen cars and stolen from cars. Neither had he robbed anyone, and he did not carry weapons, fight or hurt people. His offences were a variety of different kinds of theft, including buying or selling stolen goods. Matt's official record contained 33 offences for the previous year, all burglary related.

Media and viewing habits: Matt did not read magazines or comics, but he did read *The Sun* on a daily basis. There were two televisions available to him at the YOI, but not in his cell. In the YOI he said they also had access to a video recorder, and to satellite TV, through which they received all the movie channels and MTV. He watched two or three hours of television a day, and slightly more at weekends. His three favourite programmes were the soaps, *Home and Away, Neighbours,* and *Coronation Street,* because he could watch them regularly. He did not want to be anyone on television, but he did like Rab C Nesbitt, Bill Cosby and Roseanne, all because they were funny.

He last watched a video in the last week, but never records off the television himself. Before he was taken into custody, he would go to the cinema less than once a month. He only reported having seen one film recently, which was *The Bodyguard*, which he had seen at the cinema, with friends, once. He had no favourite films, and did not want to be anyone in films. However, he did like Arnold Schwarzenegger and Jean Claude Van Damme, because they were good action actors. He does not play computer games. There is no one in the world who he would like to be.

Case 7

Background: Alan had just turned seventeen at the time of the interview, and was living with his mother, step-father, and brother. He had been with them for three years. He had left school and was working in a factory, where he'd been for four months. One of his parents worked, the other was on invalidity benefit, after having been badly injured in a work- related accident. Alan had left school at 15. He drinks little, (and is not allowed to drink at home) and uses marijuana but no other drugs.

Offending: By his own report, Alan's current offending is fairly low (relatively), the last month having included driving illegally twice, two counts of graffiti, one stolen car and one case of buying something he knew to be stolen. His repertoire has previously included a wide range of other offences, covering many different types of theft and car crime, arson, and fighting. The police had recorded 33 offences against his name in the previous year, sixteen of which were unspecified TICs. The remainder were largely car related with one prosecution for robbery.

Media and viewing habits: Alan reads *The Sun* newspaper every day but does not read magazines or comics. He has a television in his bedroom, and the house has a video recorder, but no cable or satellite links. On the average weekday, he watches approximately four hours of television a night. Weekends involve slightly more viewing. His three favourite television programmes are *Married with Children, Neighbours* and *Home and Away,* simply because he finds them funny. He does not identify with anyone on television, nor does he particularly like anyone on television. He rented a film within 24 hours prior to the interview, which he does frequently. However, he does rarely uses the video to record off the television. He goes to the cinema less than once a month.

The five films seen most recently included *The Last Boy Scout, Universal Soldier, Marlboro Man, Stone Cold* and *Child's Play*. The first three had been viewed twice, the last two once each, and all were seen on the video at home, all with non-adult members of his family. The exception to this was *Universal Soldier*, which he viewed on his own. All were seen after 11pm in the evening.

His favourite films are *Big Boss*, and *A.W.O.L. Absent Without Leave*, both seen on videos, more than 15 times each. Generally, he particularly likes martial arts films. His mother objects to the things that he watches; he practices the moves from the kung-fu films on her. If he could be anyone in films, it would be Jean Claude Van Damme. Beyond this, the only other person he really likes who appears in films is Bruce Lee. Alan plays video games in an arcade, but infrequently. When he does play, he likes *Mortal Kombat*. No surprises in his choice of who he would like to be if he could be anyone - Jean Claude Van Damme, because he's a kung-fu expert.

Case 8

Background: Bill was sixteen, living at home with his mother, his father having died. He had left school for the summer and was working full-time, although he intended to return to studying. He had spent some time in a children's home, and claimed that he had been sent on remand to a YOI for a short period during the previous year. He had a regular girlfriend, to whom he was very attached. He drinks fairly heavily and is drunk most weekends. He reported using a variety of different drugs including hallucinogens, ecstasy and cocaine. He had been referred to a psychologist.

Offending: Bill's official offending during 1992 included 17 offences for which he had been successfully prosecuted. These were for robbery, several burglaries, handling stolen goods, and driving offences. In addition, there were alcohol and drug offences and an aggravated car theft. His range of offending was broad, with little evidence of any specialisation. He said that he had not offended for the last eight months (it was eight months since the end of 1992, where the trawl of official records ended), although he had offended heavily in the past by his own account, including many driving offences, all the different categories of theft and burglary, carrying and using weapons, fighting, buying and selling drugs, and doing criminal damage. The only thing that he denied was arson and travelling on public transport without paying his fare.

Media and viewing habits: Bill read *The Daily Mirror* two or three days a week, but no magazines or comics. He had a television in his bedroom, and a video recorder in the house, but no cable or satellite. He said that because he was working, he watched little television, none during the week or on Sundays, and only 3-4 hours in the early evening on Saturdays. Consequently, he had no favourite television programmes. If he could be anyone on television, it would be Kim Basinger's husband. He had no favourite television personalities.

He had last watched a video a few days before the interview, and rented one approximately once a week. However, he never recorded programmes off the television using the video. He went to the cinema less than once a month. The four films that he had seen most recently were *Shoot Fight, The Bodyguard, A Few Good Men*, and *Single White Female*. All of these had been seen on video, the first with his girlfriend, the rest with his mother and then subsequently his girlfriend, when he watched them for a second time. His three favourite films were *Terminator 2, Die Hard II* and *A Few Good Men*. These he had seen 15 times, 25 times and twice respectively, all on video. If he could be anyone in films he would be the actor who played Demi Moore's husband in Indecent Proposal. He had no favourite people in films. Bill played video games, at home, on a Super Nintendo, for between 10-15 hours a week. His three favourite games are *Super Mario, Streetfighter 2,* and *Zelda.*

If Bill could be anyone in the world, it would be Bruce Willis because he is married to Demi Moore. Bill's girlfriend looks, he says, very like Demi Moore. Bill's mother agreed.

Case 9

Background: Joe (nicknamed Nutter) was 16, unemployed since he left school five months before the interview. He is living with his mother and brother, where he had lived all his life. His mother works, he has no father figure. School had been a disaster area, he had difficulty with schoolwork, truanted throughout, and missed most of his last year. He had been suspended on several occasions for fighting and swearing at teachers. He gets into trouble with his group of friends from the estate and gets into fights in the pub. He drinks at the weekends, but does not use drugs.

Joe was bright and lucid, and the interviewer reported that the overriding impression of his life was of nothing to do. He knew everything there was to know about getting into cars. He was integrated into the estate's offending community, his brother 'sounds like the estate tough', and Joe guessed correctly who the next person to be interviewed on the estate was going to be. During the interview an offer of work came through, which he was happy to accept.

Offending: Joe's reports of his offending were flamboyant, including one occasion when he had been chased by the police at over 100 miles an hour, and crashed into a telegraph pole with three people in the car. He had sustained a broken jaw, broken ribs and a fractured elbow. He offends because 'I have nothing better to do, and to get money'. It becomes boring after a while. In the last month he said that he had stolen something from a car thirty times, and driven without a licence and insurance ten times. Previous offending had included the range of thefts, non-residential burglary, fighting, arson and injuring people. The official records had 63 offences in one year, of which nearly 50 were stolen cars. There was one burglary, other driving offences, one case of criminal damage and one of handling stolen goods.

Media and viewing habits: Joe reads *The Sun* most days, and the local evening paper, but no magazines or comics. The house has three television sets, of which one is in his bedroom. They have a video recorder, but no satellite or cable television. He watches an average of two to three hours every day, with slightly less on Saturday and slightly more on Sunday. His favourite television programmes reflect his interest in sport; *Sportsnight, Grand Prix,* and the soaps *Neighbours* and *Home and Away.* If he could be anyone on television, it would be Nigel Mansell, because of the cars. Apart from Mansell, he does not have any favourite people on television.

He watches videos approximately three times a week, but never uses the video to record programmes for playback. He goes to the cinema less than once a month. The films that he had seen most recently were *Paradise, Viz* and *Midnight Sting.* Each of these had been seen on video, with his brother. His only favourite film was *Rocky,* which he'd seen more than ten times on video. Consequently, if he could be anyone in films it would be Sly Stallone, but apart from Stallone there is no one else he particularly likes in films.

Joe played video games until the police confiscated his Super Nintendo because they thought it might be stolen. His favourite games were Tennis, *Streetfighter* 2 and *Super Mario.* Given the chance, he plays more than twenty hours a week.

Case 10

Background: Keith was seen in a children's home, where he had been living for five months. He was fourteen at the time of interview. Before this, he had been in another children's home. He had been in care almost continuously since the age of seven, with a short break when he was thirteen when he went home to his mother. His primary caregiver is his keyworker in the children's home, but he was in contact with his mother, who was unemployed. He hoped to become a footballer, as he was good at it, or, if this did not work out, he wanted to become a social worker. He was attending school but his truanting levels were high and he had been both suspended and excluded for sniffing gas and hitting a teacher. He was first arrested when he was eleven for a fight at the children's home, when someone else called the police. He rarely drinks more than two cans of beer a week. He uses marijuana regularly.

Offending: Exceptionally, Keith does not drive, although he can steal cars. He steals them and others drive them. He offends for 'the buzz' and for the money. Burglaries are his favourite as he enjoys spending the money. In the last month, he said that he had stolen from shops (three times), from cars (once), threatened someone with a weapon (once), bought drugs (three times), damaged things (once, and 30 counts of graffitti) got into a fight, and hurt someone enough to cause injury (once). This was his usual repertoire. As well as avoiding driving offences, he did not steal from people, nor did he buy or sell stolen goods. There were 22 offences against his name, mostly burglary, with some handling of stolen goods and some criminal damage in a children's home.

Media and viewing habits: Reflecting his interest in sport, Keith reads *Match*, and *Shoot*, and also reads the *Daily Express* every day, together with the local evening paper. There are two televisions at the home, but none in his bedroom. They also have a video recorder. He watches a lot of television, up to six hours a day including Saturdays and Sundays, up to 11pm. His favourite programmes are *The Bill*, any sport programme such as *Grandstand*, and *Eastenders*. The first he enjoys because he likes seeing other criminals. The last he likes because it is just like real life.

He would not wish to be anyone on television, but he does particularly like Ryan Giggs, 'the best footballer out'. He sees videos regularly, more than once a week, but never records programmes off the television. He goes to the cinema two or three times a month. The films he had seen most recently included *The Bodyguard*, *Terminator 2*, *Cliffhanger* and *The Unforgiven*. All except *Cliffhanger* were seen on video, with other people in the children's home. He went to the cinema for *Cliffhanger* with friends. He has seen *Terminator 2* ten times, the others were only viewed once or twice.

Terminator 2 also featured as his favourite film, followed by *Robocop* (also viewed ten times) and *Stir Crazy*, seen three times. Unusually, he went on to name a fourth favourite film, *Planes, Trains and Automobiles* which he had seen twice. All these had been viewed on video. He did not identify with anyone in films, but had three people he particularly liked: Gene Wilder, John Candy and Richard Pryor, because they made him laugh. He played video games in an arcade, and had a Commodore at home which he never used. He played for less than five hours a week, and particularly liked *Streetfighter, Italia '90* and *Mortal Kombat*.

Case 11

Background: Ben was seventeen at the time of interview, living with his sister and brother-in-law, and their children, where he had been for a month since leaving home. He had left school the previous year, and had been unemployed for sixteen months. His sister's family were present throughout the interview, keeping it fairly light in tone (his brother-in-law commented that he did not get all this attention when he was arrested for stealing buses in 1976). Ben did not know whether his mother worked, and had little contact with his father. In his last year of school he went to the engineering class but nothing else. He was suspended for throwing a chair at a teacher. He drinks infrequently, and does not use drugs.

Offending: Ben was clear that he offended for money, not for enjoyment. He did not enjoy stealing cars but did it so that he could sell the wheels. Moving to his sister's in the last month had been a turning point and he had not offended since; he now had something for which it was worth keeping out of custody - his sister and her children and a decent home. By his account, his offending in the past had included driving illegally, stealing from shops, homes and cars, stealing cars, trespassing, carrying a weapon, and fighting.

The 27 officially recorded offences corroborated his account, including thefts and driving offences. There was one count of actual bodily harm, and one of carrying an offensive weapon.

Media and viewing habits: He did not read magazines or comics, and only read the local evening paper a few days a week. There were five television sets in his sister's house, one of which was in his bedroom. They also had a video recorder, but no satellite or cable. He watched approximately four or five hours every day, between 6pm and 11pm. His favourite television programmes were *The A-Team, Baywatch, Gladiators,* and *Soldier Soldier*. The first he enjoyed because they were 'always making and repairing stuff', the last because there was a lot of fighting. His sister's partner did not approve of him watching *Soldier Soldier*. He wouldn't want to be anyone on television but he did like the wrestlers, because 'it's a laugh'. He rarely watches videos (less than once a month), but records *The A-Team* off the television once a week. He used to have a full collection.

Ben goes to the cinema once a month, and only the first of his five most recently seen films was seen at the cinema; the rest were viewed on television. They were *Super Mario Bros, Lethal Weapon II, Die Hard, Beverley Hills Cop* and *Back to the Future*. Most of these were seen between 9pm and 11pm, and most with his family. The first was seen with his girlfriend. His two favourite films were *Die Hard* (seen three times) and *Beverley Hills Cop* (seen fifteen times), both on videos at friends' houses most of the time. Again, he would not want to be anyone in films, but he did like Bruce Willis and Eddie Murphy, the former because he could be funny.

He played video games at home, on a SEGA Master System. He used to have a SEGA Mega Drive but he had sold it. He enjoys *Cool Sport, Columns,* and *Super Mario Bros*. His sister disapproves; she doesn't like the noise.

Case 12

Background: Gavin had just turned sixteen, and had left school. He said he was waiting for college to start. He had spent some time in a YOI earlier in the year, but was now living with his mother (who was divorced) and his own partner, in his family home. He had a long history with social services, and had spent time in children's homes and other YOIs. He had disappeared for weeks at a time, and absconded regularly from Local Authority custody. In the previous year he had lived in seven different places. He regularly took hallucinogens, every other day, he claimed. His partner was pregnant with his child, which he claimed would calm him down.

Offending: Gavin was part of an offending family, both his brother and his father being heavily involved. His official 1992 offences included nine offences for which he had been successfully prosecuted, and ten that had been taken into consideration. Three offences had been withdrawn, including a particularly nasty one involving cruelty to an animal. Most of his offences were residential burglary, with one stolen car and one attempted theft from a car. He had also been convicted of ABH, relating to a burglary when he had disturbed the injured person. The interviewer commented on his lack of distinction between public and private property, and on his knowledge of the legal system.

By his own account, he was a very frequent offender indeed, the last month containing twenty counts of illegal driving, two of buying or selling stolen goods, thirty of carrying a weapon (all the time) and thirty of buying drugs. He admitted to having committed the whole range of offences at some time in his life, from burglaries through thefts and robbery to fighting. The interviewer felt that this was quite possibly an exaggeration and that he was proud of his history.

Media and viewing habits: Gavin was not interested in answering these questions, and it was difficult to encourage him to concentrate. He read *Smash Hits*, but nothing else. There were four television sets in the house, one in his bedroom. Most days he watched 3-4 hours,

Saturdays he would not watch at all. He claimed that he did not have any favourite programmes, and he didn't know who he would want to be on television, and he had no favourite people. He had recently viewed a video, which he did more than once a week, although he never recorded programmes from the television. Neither did he go to the cinema. The only film he could remember seeing recently was *Total Recall* which he had seen on video, alone the first time, with his girlfriend and mother on the second occasion. In total he had seen it five times. It was also one of his favourite films, the other two being *The Hidden* (seen three times) and *The Last Action Hero* (seen once), both viewed on video. If he could be anyone in films it would be Arnold Schwarzenegger, because of his 'muscles' and the 'action'. Apart from Schwarzenegger, there were no other people he particularly liked.

He did play computer games, at home on a Commodore, for between 5 and 10 hours a week. His favourite games were *Sonic II*, *Super Mario Bros* and *Streetfighter*. His mother complained because he was wasting his time.

Case 13

Background: Paul was a fifteen year old boy interviewed in a YOI, where he had been for three months. Before this he had spent periods in children's homes and at home with his family. Both his parents work. His girlfriend, who was several years older than he, was expecting his child. He was reasonably happy in the YOI apart from missing her, although he believed that he was throwing his life away. His one and only ambition was to become a disc jockey. He was attending the YOI educational facility, but when he had been at regular school he had missed a great deal, and had been excluded for throwing a chair at a teacher. He did not drink a great deal (and none in custody) but did take a range of drugs including using magic mushrooms and ecstasy.

Offending: Paul had been driving since he was nine. He said that he had been involved in shoplifting, criminal damage, stealing cars, ram raiding and burglaries. He also admitted to buying and selling stolen goods, buying and selling drugs, arson and injury. His official record included 22 offences for 1992, including burglary and arson (at school), criminal damage, and common assault against a police officer.

Media and viewing habits: Paul did not read newpapers or magazines, but he did enjoy *The Beano* and *The Dandy*. The YOI Unit on which he was placed had one television, to which they were allowed access at certain times of the day. He watched approximately two hours a day, and it was whatever anyone else had put on. He only had one favourite programme, *The Bill*, although he did say that if he could be anyone on television it would be someone in *Home and Away*. He also liked Jasper Carrott, and any other comedians. They view videos in the YOI, he claimed this was approximately once a day. The only one he could remember seeing recently was *The Running Man*. His favourite film was *Child's Play*, of which he had seen all three parts, and which at one point he had seen as frequently as three times a week (when not in custody). He liked it because he found the way the toy walked and talked amusing, and liked the way he comes to life. His girlfriend's mother disapproved of him seeing *Child's Play*, but if he could be anyone on television, this is the film he would like to be in, although he did not specify a character.

Other people he liked in films were Arnold Schwarzenegger and Rambo, for 'the action'. He played video games, but he found them boring. He wouldn't have described them as favourites, but he played *Terminator* and a *Racing Car Game* of some sort. He played these in arcades when he was not in custody.

Conclusion

These case studies of frequent offenders illustrate several of the themes emerging from the previous chapters and provide some more general impression of the backgrounds and lifestyles of these types of offenders. It is within this context that their viewing habits have to be assessed. The first thing to note is that there is no single 'type' of offender, and that frequent offenders are, in some respects at least, a heterogenous group. Within this group of 13, there were those who were working full-time, those hoping to continue studying, those who were unemployed. Some were living with their families, some were in local authority custody, some in the custody of the prison service, and one with his own partner. Secondly, even in these brief case descriptions, the high level of disruption and movement in these young people's lives emerges clearly. Many very frequent offenders will have had extensive contact with social services for welfare as well as offending reasons, many will have spent time in care, in custody or with family members other than parents. Their lifestyles were obviously very different from those of the average schoolchild, and the level of their offending was presumably fairly time consuming. In addition, they reported relatively high levels of drug and alcohol use. Against this background, their choices of television programmes and films were conservative and predictable. The films they liked were mainstream, their general interest in television and broadcast media was not high. There was nothing that stood out in dramatic contrast to the description of the viewing habits of comparison schoolchildren described in earlier chapters. They also had difficulty in remembering things seen recently. In particular, they either did not like or could not answer the questions concerning characters who they admired or would like to be.

Notes
1. See Hagell, A. and Newburn, T. (1994) *Persistent Young Offenders*, London: PSI, for a fuller discussion of the problems inherent in identifying 'persistent' offenders.

Chapter 7   **Summary and Conclusions**

Discussions of juvenile offending and the media have tended to assume that the viewing habits of juvenile offenders are different from those of their non-offending peers. However, very little basic information exists concerning the television, video and cinema habits of juvenile offenders, and this study was designed to go some way towards filling that gap. This study, based on a descriptive analysis of what a small (yet representative sample) of frequent juvenile offenders chose to watch reveals some interesting similarities between these offenders and a representative sample of schoolchildren. Given the nature of this research, it is not possible on the basis of the data collected to do more than describe and compare viewing habits and preferences. It is not within the scope of this study to consider the issue of possible links between viewing habits and offending behaviour - that task must be left to other research.

The study made comparisons between two very different groups of children. The first were a group of 78 male and female juvenile offenders, who had all been arrested <u>at least three times</u> within one year, and who had or were alleged to have committed an average of ten offences each within 1992. The second was a group of over five hundred male and female schoolchildren, drawn at random from a wide range of schools in England and Wales. Given that the questionnaire was administered in schools towards the end of the summer term, in most cases after exams were over, the schoolchildren were most likely to be those who were regular attenders and, thus, most unlike the sample of offenders. Consequently, it is our view that were it the case that young offenders' viewing habits were significantly different from those of young people in general, it is likely that they would have been revealed by the comparisons made in this study.

Key Findings

- Reading of comics, magazines and newspapers was more common amongst the schoolchildren than the offenders. If they read papers, tabloid newspapers were the most frequent choice by all the children. Larger proportions of offenders than schoolchildren reported that they did not read anything. Within both samples, few young people claimed to be reading titles that have been the subject of public concern. Their interests were largely in sport and music among the boys, and fashion among the girls.

- The offenders had less access to television, video and other equipment than the comparison schoolchildren, reporting fewer televisions, fewer video recorders, and less access to non-terrestrial broadcasting in the places where they were living.

- There was a very slight overall trend for the offenders to report more television viewing over the week, but this was balanced by the fact that a larger proportion of the offenders than the schoolchildren reported that they watched <u>no</u> television at all.

- The two groups were watching equal amounts of television directly after the 9pm watershed. However, the offenders were more likely than the schoolchildren to be watching beyond 11pm at night.

- A lower proportion of offenders than comparison schoolchildren were able to name any favourite television programmes.

- Of those who had a favourite, the most popular television programme amongst the male offenders was *The Bill*. In addition, they enjoyed *Eastenders, Neighbours, Home and Away* and *Prisoner Cell Block H*. The female offenders listed much the same soap operas as amongst their favourite television programmes.

- Among the schoolchildren, the equivalent choices were very similar, with the exception that the schoolgirls did not mention *Prisoner Cell Block H*, and the schoolboys were less likely to name *The Bill*. The most popular programmes for the schoolgirls and the schoolboys were *Home and Away* and *Neighbours* respectively.

- The offenders had difficulty in identifying anyone on television they would like to be. However, within all groups, offenders and schoolchildren alike, Arnold Schwarzenegger was a common choice.

- Video film viewing was very common in both groups. Where their video behaviour differed, it was in time-shift viewing; few offenders recorded programmes and then watched them at a different time, in contrast to the schoolchildren.

- Cinema attendance was quite high in both groups, though the schoolchildren reported higher rates of attendance than the offenders. Half of the offenders said that they rarely or never went to the cinema compared to a quarter of the schoolchildren.

- Reports of which films had been viewed most recently resulted in a wide range of recently released films and videos. The film most frequently reported as the latest seen was *Jurassic Park* (certificate PG) for the male offenders, and *Terminator 2* (certificate 15) for the schoolboys. For both groups, their favourite film was *Terminator 2*. Within the top five favourite films, both the schoolboys and the male offenders named three films that were released for general viewing with 18 certificates and two released with a 15 certificate. (Very few of either group were actually 18 years old.)

- Offenders who had been convicted of violent offences did not have any particular viewing habits or preferences distinguishable from the group as a whole.

- Computer games were popular and commonly played within all samples, girls and boys. There was no difference in whether or not the two samples reported playing games (although once again, the offenders had less access to their own equipment), and such a wide variety of games were reported that it was difficult to draw any firm conclusions concerning types of games played. The most popular games among the offenders and the schoolchildren were *Streetfighter 1* and 2, and *Sonic I and II*.

- In terms of a general measure of 'media use' (frequency of newspaper reading, and degree of engagement with television, cinema, video and computer games) offenders and schoolchildren registered similar mean scores.

- It is important to bear in mind the different lifestyles and socio-economic status of the young offenders, resulting in less access to equipment, fewer chances to view alone, and different use of their time and interests, all of which will have repercussions on their attachment to and use of various different media.

These results suggest that, at least in terms of their viewing habits, juvenile offenders are not easily distinguishable from schoolchildren of the same age, except that they may have restricted access to equipment, less chance to control what they watch, and less chance to view on their own. They are very similar in their habits and preferences to the majority of ordinary schoolchildren. Of course, some juvenile offenders are ordinary schoolchildren. From the interviews and the survey conducted as part of this study, there was little evidence of any particular interests or preferences that were restricted to the offenders. Any variation between the groups only ever applied to one or two offenders or schoolchildren. In both groups, they did not report anything in the way of unusual programmes or films, their choices being largely very mainstream. There was certainly no evidence of any particular attraction to programmes or films with an especially violent content - or, more accurately, the offenders do not appear to be any more attracted to violent television programmes or films than are most children of their age. This is not to say that youngsters were not attracted to violent films, clearly they were, but rather that it was the broader context of 'action', which often included violence, that tended to characterise offenders' choices. Where there were specific interests among the offenders, for example in their choice of *The Bill* as their favourite television programme, this appeared to reflect issues that were perhaps closely related to their experiences. The programme was popular with the schoolchildren and the offenders, but its high ranking by the offenders should not be surprising given the centrality of the police as an organisation in their lives, and the realism with which the programme attempts to portray the working of that organisation and the experiences of those that come into contact with it. Indeed, it was soap operas and their high excitement and high action cinematic equivalents that dominated the preferences of the vast majority of the children in both samples. The case studies highlighted the fact that young offenders' viewing habits need to be assessed in the light of their lifestyles, and that offending and media habits are both single elements in a complicated kaleidoscope of background and behaviour.

Further research

The exploratory and descriptive nature of this small study leads inevitably to major limitations on the conclusions that can be drawn from it. The fact that these offenders did not watch more television, and did not appear to select more violent programmes or films than schoolchildren generally, might lead one to question the assumption that it is the volume of viewing of such programmes and films that leads a vulnerable minority to offend. If anything, this study would suggest that juveniles who offend frequently are less engaged with television, cinema and video than their school peers. Of course, this is not to say that their viewing habits were not significantly different at some earlier point in their childhoods, and it remains the case that further research might help to establish a more developmental understanding of the role and place of media consumption during the early lifespan and its possible relationship to offending behaviour.

One major limitation of the project was that it relied on self-report data, and on only one kind of self-report data. Presenting children with lists of films, rather than prompting them to list films themselves, might have resulted in a different picture. The role of memory in biasing reports of viewing habits is likely to be a very important factor. A second limitation was that this study was restricted to children over the age of eleven. A third was the size of the offending sample which, whilst representative of frequent offenders, was nonetheless small. Research with different age groups is obviously essential, and research using different samples is needed to take into account the distinction between frequent offenders and serious offenders. Alternative research methodologies, including the use of in-depth interviews, would aid further exploration of some of the questions raised by this project. The viewing behaviour of offenders needs to be understood both in the light of the psychology of cognitive and moral development and taking into account the social circumstances of the lives of the young children in question. Crucially, studies of what offenders watch need to be supplemented by research which examines how they watch and how they understand what they see.

Appendix 1

     LEISURE ACTIVITIES SURVEY

The purpose of this research is to look at what programmes and films young people are watching on video and television.
This survey is taking place in a large number of schools and the answers we get will be added together and analysed by computer. No schools or individuals will be identified.

Your answers are *totally confidential*.

To answer the questions either tick the answer(s) in the boxes that apply to you, or put your reply in the spaces provided. If anything is unclear the teacher should be able to help.

1.   **Are you?**
          Male .... ☐
          Female .... ☐

2.   **How old are you?**
                    .... years

3.   **In this space below please put the names of any comics or magazines that you read *regularly*?**
          1. .... ☐
          2. .... ☐
          3. .... ☐
          4. .... ☐
          5. .... ☐

4.   **How often do you read a newspaper?**
                                          Tick one box only
          Every day .... ☐
          More than once a week .... ☐
          Once a week .... ☐
          Less than once a week .... ☐
          Hardly ever/never .... ☐
          Don't know .... ☐

5.   If you read a newspaper, which one do you tend to read?

Tick one box only

Daily Express .... ☐
Daily Telegraph .... ☐
Guardian .... ☐
Independent .... ☐
Mail .... ☐
Mirror .... ☐
Star .... ☐
Sun .... ☐
Times .... ☐
Today .... ☐
Other (please say which) .... ☐
....

6.   How many television sets do you have in your home?

....

7.   Do you have a television in your bedroom?

Yes .... ☐
No .... ☐

8.   Which of these do you have in your home?

Tick all that apply

Video recorder .... ☐
Radio .... ☐
CD/record/cassette player .... ☐
Cable TV .... ☐
Satellite TV receiver .... ☐

9.   Which channels can you get via cable/satellite?

Tick all that apply

Sky Movies Plus .... ☐
Sky Movies Gold .... ☐
The Movie Channel .... ☐
Other (please say which) .... ☐
....

10. We would like to know when you watch television. Looking at the time periods below, during which periods did you watch television last week? Please put a tick against the times and days that you watched television.

	6.30am-1pm	1pm-6pm	6pm-9pm	9pm-11pm	11pm-6.30am	Didn't watch
Average weekday						
Saturday						
Sunday						

11. Now think about the amount of time you spent watching television last week. For each day please tick how many hours TV you watched.

	Average weekday	Saturday	Sunday
None			
Less than 1 hour			
1 hour-2 hours			
2 hours-3 hours			
3 hours-4 hours			
4 hours-5 hours			
5 hours-6 hours			
6 hours or more			

12. We would like to know what your favourite television programmes are. Please write the names of up to five below.

   1. ....
   2. ....
   3. ....
   4. ....
   5. ....

13. If you has the chance to be someone on television, who would you choose to be?

   ....

   Why?

14.   Who are your favourite people on television?

1. ....

2. ....

3. ....

15.   When did you last watch a video?

Tick one box only

Earlier today/yesterday .... ☐
Within the last three days .... ☐
Within the last week .... ☐
Within the last two weeks .... ☐
Within the last month .... ☐
Longer ago than that .... ☐

16.   How often do you watch films from a video shop or club?

Tick one box only

More than once a week .... ☐
Once a week .... ☐
2-3 times a month .... ☐
Once a month .... ☐
Less than once a month .... ☐
Hardly ever/never .... ☐
Don't know .... ☐

17.   How often do you use your video recorder to watch programmes recorded earlier off TV?

Tick one box only

Four or more times a week .... ☐
Two or three times a week .... ☐
About once a week .... ☐
Less often than once a week .... ☐
Never .... ☐

What sort of programmes do you record?

....

18.   How often do you go to the cinema?

Tick one box only

More than once a week .... ☐
Once a week .... ☐
2-3 times a month .... ☐
Once a month .... ☐
Less than once a month .... ☐
Hardly ever/never .... ☐
don't know .... ☐

19. **Please write the names of up to five films you have seen on video or at the cinema recently. Then please say whether you think anyone would have disapproved of you seeing that film.**

	Where did you see the film?		Would anybody have disapproved?	
Title of film	Cinema	Video	No	Yes
Film 1	☐	☐	☐	☐
Film 2	☐	☐	☐	☐
Film 3	☐	☐	☐	☐
Film 4	☐	☐	☐	☐
Film 5	☐	☐	☐	☐

Who did you watch each of these films with? *(Tick all that apply)*

Film 1   Alone ☐   Parents ☐   Other adults ☐   Other family ☐   Friends ☐

Film 2   Alone ☐   Parents ☐   Other adults ☐   Other family ☐   Friends ☐

Film 3   Alone ☐   Parents ☐   Other adults ☐   Other family ☐   Friends ☐

Film 4   Alone ☐   Parents ☐   Other adults ☐   Other family ☐   Friends ☐

Film 5   Alone ☐   Parents ☐   Other adults ☐   Other family ☐   Friends ☐

---

20. **Please tell us the names of your favourite films and how many times you have seen them.**

No of times watched

1. .... ☐
2. .... ☐
3. .... ☐

---

21. **If you could be someonewho appears in films, who would you be?**

....

Why?

---

22. **Please put the names of any other people in films who you particularly like**

1 ....
2 ....
3 ....

What is it you like about this person/these people?

23.   Do you play video/computer games?

Yes .... ☐
No .... ☐

If Yes, what are your favourite games?

1 ....

2 ....

3 ....

24.   Where do you play them?

Tick one box only

In an arcade .... ☐
At home .... ☐
At a friend's house .... ☐
Other (please state) .... ☐

....

25.   Do you have a videogame console or a computer?
Yes .... ☐
No .... ☐

26.   In a typical week how much time do you spend playing computer games?

0-5 hours .... ☐
6-10 hours .... ☐
11-15 hours .... ☐
16-20 hours .... ☐
Over 20 hours .... ☐

27.   Does anyone disaapprove of you playing computer games?
No .... ☐
Yes .... ☐
If Yes, who? ....
What do they disapprove of?

28.   If you had the chance to be anybody who would you be?

....

Why?

Appendix 2

VIEWING HABITS INTERVIEW

Summer 1993

ID NUMBER...........................

Schedule ref: TN/4 June 1993

1.　**Which magazines or comics do you read regularly?**

　　1. ....
　　2. ....
　　3. ....
　　4. ....
　　5. ....

2.　**How often do you read a newspaper?**

Nearly every day/every day	1
Four to five days a week	2
Two to three days a week	3
Once a week	4
Hardly ever/never	5
Don't know	9

3.　**Which newspaper do you most often read?**

Daily Express	1
Daily Telegraph	2
Guardian	3
Independent	4
Mail	5
Mirror	6
Sport	7
Star	8
Sun	10
Times	11
Today	12
Local evening paper	13
Other (please state)	

　　..

4.　**How many television sets do you have where you are currently living?**

5.　**Do you have a television in your bedroom?**

No	0
Yes	1

6. **Which if any of the following do you have in your home?**
(0=No   1=Yes)

Video recorder
Radio
CD/record/cassette player
Cable TV
Satellite TV receiver

---

7. **Which channels can you receive via cable/satellite?**

Sky Movies Plus	1
Sky Movies Gold	2
The Movie Channel	3
Other (please specify)	

....

---

8. **Looking at the time periods on this card, during which periods did you yourself watch television last week? Weekend**

And what about Saturday?
And what about Sunday?

	6.30am -1pm	1pm- 6pm	6pm- 9pm	9pm- 11pm	11pm -6.30	Didn't watch
Weekday						
Saturday						
Sunday						

9. **Now thinking about the amount of time you spent watching television last week, about how many hours of television did you watch on a weekday?**
And Saturday?   And Sunday?

	Average Weekday	Saturday	Sunday
Less than 1 hour			
1 hour-2 hours			
2 hours-3 hours			
3 hours-4 hours			
4 hours-5 hours			
5 hours-6 hours			
6 hours or more			
None			

10. **And was that a typical week or did you watch more or less television than usual?**

More.....1   Less.....2   Same.....3

---

11. **Would you tell me the names of your five favourite television programmes?**

1. ....
2. ....
3. ....
4. ....
5. ....

---

12. **What is it that you enjoy about these programmes? (VERBATIM— only cover two or three favourites)**

....
....
....
....
....

---

13. **If you had the chance to be someone who appears on television,. who would you choose to be?**

....

PROBE FOR WHY?

....
....
....

---

14. **Who are your favourite people who appear on television? (ie anybody else?)**

1. ....
2. ....
3. ....

PROBE FOR WHY?

....
....
....

---

15. When did you last watch a video?

Earlier today/yesterday	1
Within the last three days	2
Within the last week	3
Within the last two weeks	4
Within the last month	5
Longer ago than that	6

16. How often do you watch films from a video shop or club?

More than once a week	1
Once a week	2
2-3 times a month	3
Once a month	4
Less than once a month	5
Hardly ever/never	6
Don't know	9

17. How often do you use your video recorder to watch programmes recorded earlier off TV?

Four or more times a week	1
Two or three times a week	2
About once a week	3
Less often than once a week	4
Never	5

PROBE FOR WHAT SORT OF PROGRAMMES

....

....

....

18. How often do you go to the cinema?

More than once a week	1
Once a week	2
2-3 times a month	3
Once a month	4
Less than once a month	5
Hardly ever/never	6
Don't know	9

(CODE THE ANSWERS TO QUESTION 19 IN THE GRID BELOW)

19.   Which films (cinema or video) have you seen recently? (up to 5)

THE PROBE FOR

– Where they saw the film?

– What time of day they saw the film?

– Who they were with when they saw the film?

– How many times they have seen the film?

Title of Film	Time viewed	Where viewed			Who with			Times viewed(No.)
1.								
2.								
3.								
4.								
5.								

CODES

Time

1	2	3	4	5	6
6.30am -1pm	1pm-6pm	6pm-9pm	9pm-11pm	11pm-6.30	Didn't watch

Where 1=on TV   2=on video where currently living   3=on video at a friend's house   4=cinema   5=other (please specify)

(Record all)

Who with   0=alone   1=parents   2=other adults   3=other family (non-adult)   4=friends   5=other (please specify) ENTER ALL THAT APPLY)

20.   What are your favourite films? (up to 3)

THEN PROBE FOR

–Where they saw the film?

–How many times they have seen the film?

Title of Film	Where viewed			No. of Times viewed
1.				
2.				
3.				

CODES

Where 1=on TV   2=on video where currently living   3=on video at a friend's house   4=cinema   5=other (please specify)

21. **Does anyone ever disapprove of anything that you watch?** NO=0
                                                                    YES=1

   If YES, Who? ....

   What do they disapprove of? ....

   ....

---

22. **If you had the chance to be someone who appears in films, who would you choose to be?**

   ....

   PROBE FOR WHY?

   ....

   ....

   ....

---

23. **Are there any other people who appear in films who you particularly like?**

   1 ....

   2 ....

   3 ....

   PROBE FOR WHY

   ....

   ....

   ....

---

24. **Do you play video/computer games?**   Yes=1   No=2

   If Yes, what are your favourite games?

   1 ....

   2 ....

   3 ....

---

25. **Where do you play them?**

   In an arcade   1

   At home   2

   At a friend's house   3

   Other (please state) ....

26. **What type of videogame consoles or computers do you have?**

Atari	1
Commodore	2
SEGA Mega Drive	3
SEGA Master System	4
Super Nintendo	5
Nintendo Game Boy	6

Other (please specify) ....

27. **In a typical week, how much time would you spend playing computer games?**

1=0-5hrs   2=5-10hrs   3=10-15hrs   4=15-20hrs   5=20+

28. **Does anyone disapprove of you playing computer games?**

No	0
Yes	1

IF YES: Who? ....
....
....

29. **If you had the chance to be ANYBODY, who would you be?**

....

PROBE FOR WHY?
....

....

....

....

....

....

Appendix 3

Film	Video	Description
BRITISH BOARD OF FILM CLASSIFICATION		
Feature film and video classifications		
Film	Video	Description
U	U, Uc	Universal: Particularly suitable for young children.
PG	PG	Parental Guidance: some scenes may be unsuitable for young children.
12	–	Suitable only for persons of 12 years and over.
15	15	Suitable only for persons of 15 years and over.
18	18	Suitable only for persons of 18 years and over.